BREAKING THE SPELL
OF DISENCHANTMENT

Mystery, Meaning, and Metaphysics
in the Work of C. G. Jung

Roderick Main

Zurich Lecture Series in Analytical Psychology

ISAPZURICH

Volume 8

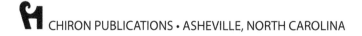

CHIRON PUBLICATIONS · ASHEVILLE, NORTH CAROLINA

www.ChironPublications.com

Interior and cover design by Danijela Mijailovic
Printed primarily in the United States of America.

Cover image from THE RED BOOK by C.G. Jung, edited by Sonu Shamdasani, translated by Mark Kyburz, John Peck, and Sonu Shamdasani. Copyright © 2009 by the Foundation of the Works of C. G. Jung. Translation copyright (c) 2009 by Mark Kyburz, John Peck, and Sonu Shamdasani. Used by permission of W. W. Norton & Company, Inc.

978-1-68503-076-6 paperback
978-1-68503-077-3 hardcover
978-1-68503-078-0 ebook
978-1-68503-079-7 CreateSpace

Library of Congress Cataloging-in-Publication Data Pending

"In the wake of the Great Reset (and the great resignation), hardly any topic could be more urgent than disenchantment. In this fascinating monograph, Roderick Main carefully and meticulously delineates the contours of the phenomenon of disenchantment, and then goes further — assessing the possibilities of reversing (or transcending) this catastrophic decline. On Main's compelling account, the project of analytical psychology involves nothing less than the 'rebirth' of Western culture — and a reinvestment of magic into a meaningful dimension of existence. This highly recommended book deserves to find many readers across numerous disciplines, both clinical and academic, and it paves the way for the long-awaited return to the contemporary discourse of the arts and humanities of Jung as a major theoretical and conceptual player."

Professor Paul Bishop, William Jacks Chair in Modern Languages, University of Glasgow

CONTENTS

In memory of
Katherine ("Catriona") Helen Main (1935–2016)
and
Donald McIntosh Main (1964–2016)

PREFACE

In 1982, after my first year as an undergraduate studying Classics at the University of Oxford, I dropped out of formal education and went to live in Glastonbury, where I explored magic and wrote poetry. This was probably not a very wise thing to do, considering the life skills, or lack of them, that I had at the time. It was, however, an expression of my sense that the education I had been receiving, brilliant though it was in its own way, was too focused on developing narrow, specialist knowledge and skills aimed at impressing the intellect and securing a career. It was missing, or at any rate I was at that time unable to find in it, something I considered crucial: a vital connection to the mystery, meaningfulness, and sacredness of reality. In the terms I shall be exploring in this book, I felt that at Oxford I had entered a disenchanted milieu, and, in leaving to pursue magic and poetry, I was seeking reenchantment—something to enchant and to chant—in a quite literal way.

Although I eventually returned to Oxford, completed my degree, undertook a PhD in Religious Studies at Lancaster University, and—following a far from uncheckered path—have ended up working in a university myself, the tension between the predominantly disenchanted world of academia and another world of mystery, meaning, and sacredness has remained continually with me. This tension is, I believe, encapsulated in the subject matter I am fortunate to be able to research and teach in the Department of Psychosocial and Psychoanalytic Studies at the University of Essex: Jungian psychology, including my own specialism (yes, specialism) of synchronicity.

When I was invited to deliver the 2021 Zurich Lecture Series and was seeking a topic on which to speak, I eventually settled on disenchantment and its undoing. This topic epitomizes what I have been doing throughout my professional life, namely, exploring the relationship between disenchanted modernity and attempts, mainly Jung's, to question that vision of modernity. Thinking about this issue in the context of a university is apt, since Max Weber's most famous statements about the disenchantment of the modern world occur in a lecture, "Science as a Vocation," delivered to students who might be considering an academic career. Moreover, if there is a place where the concomitants of dis-enchantment—intellectualization, rationalization, and bureaucratization—especially flourish, it is in modern universities. I am grateful for the spur and opportunity provided by the lecture invitation to think about all these matters further.

Ironically, the first time I used the term "reenchantment" ("dis-enchantment" was still a step too far) in the title of one of my publications was at the suggestion of a colleague in the Department of Sociology who was concerned that, without this reference to the thought of Weber, my work might not be deemed submissible to the Sociology panel of the (very disenchanting) Research Assessment Exercise in which UK universities were then engaged. In satisfying the bureaucratic requirement, I also happily lit upon one of the themes that would guide much of my work over the ensuing years.

The concept of disenchantment captures, so I shall argue in this book, the cultural condition, or at least narrative, to which Jung's work was largely responding. The term also connects Jung's predominantly psychological project with sociological discourses—again, very apt for me considering my academic location within a department of psychosocial and psycho-analytic studies.

I have titled my book *Breaking the Spell of Disenchantment* to flag that disenchantment, as well as being a process that can free us from naïve en-chantments, is an enchantment of its own, a narrative with a tremendously powerful, and in some ways strangling, grip on modern Western culture. Jung's work, I believe, provides resources for at least loosening that grip—something that can be relevant as much at a clinical as at a cultural level.

Readers of the following pages will find a fair amount of intellectualization and rationalization in my academic style. I try to justify this on the grounds that genuine reenchantment presupposes and enfolds, rather than retreats from, the process of disenchantment. I can't promise always—or indeed ever—to have found my way to the other side of disenchantment, but I hope my struggles in that direction will at least help to highlight some of the issues of engaging with this powerful topic.

In Chapter 1, I discuss what is meant by disenchantment and what have been some of the main cultural and scholarly responses to the notion. We shall find that the picture is a complex and multifaceted one but that an overall set of propositions implied by disenchantment can be identified and used as a lens through which to examine Jung's work. In this chapter, I shall also provide an overview of Jung's response to disenchantment. I argue that his work overall attempts to undo disenchantment and its perceived negative consequences—in other words, to "reenchant the world." However, it does this in a way that views reenchantment as part of an overarching recursive process that also essentially and perpetually involves both disenchantment and naïve enchantment—even if the reenchanting aspect of the process arguably has the greatest need to be foregrounded in the present cultural moment. I also argue that Jung's late account of individuation in *Mysterium Coniunctionis*, which sees it as culminating in experience of mystical union with the divine (*unio mystica*), connects surprisingly with hints in Max Weber's writing that such mystical experience can provide a potential way out of disenchantment.

Considering the special importance of the transition from disenchantment to reenchantment, I explore more closely in the remaining chapters Jung's responses to the seeming absence of mystery, meaning, and relationship to spiritual reality that characterizes disenchantment. These are the *Mystery, Meaning, and Metaphysics in the Work of C. G. Jung* of my subtitle. In relation to the purported absence of mystery, I review in Chapter 2 Jung's lifelong experience, observation, and study of anomalous (or "paranormal") phenomena, which raise question marks over narrow conceptions of empiricism and reason. In relation to the question of meaning, I examine in Chapter 3 Jung's statements implying that meaning is not just subjectively projected onto a meaningless external reality but can be an inherent feature discoverable in, or creatively emergent from, the one reality that we also are. Finally, in relation to the claimed unbridgeable separation between the world and any transcendent reality, I consider in Chapter 4 an implicit, psychologically disguised metaphysics identifiable in Jung's work, which supports an intimate and mutually transformative relationship between the world and the divine.

Informing Jung's engagements with disenchantment in each of these areas was his profound concern with psychological wholeness. The book is informed throughout by the vision of Jung's work as a particularly rich and distinctive form of holistic thought, valuable not only for psychotherapy but also for providing a critical perspective on some of our current social, political, and environmental crises, insofar as these have roots in the still prevalent story of disenchantment.

ACKNOWLEDGMENTS

I should like to thank Murray Stein and his colleagues at the International School of Analytical Psychology, Zurich, and at Chiron Publications for the invitation to present the 2021 Zurich Lecture Series and to write this associated book. Restrictions relating to the COVID-19 pandemic had just eased sufficiently for the lectures to take place in person, and I was deeply moved by the warm and generous hospitality I received in Zurich amid the lingering precautions. The invitation provided a timely spur to draw together and further develop my thoughts on the book's topic, with which I have been grappling for years. Though completing the book has been a lengthy, alas tardy, process, without this spur I should have been unlikely to have been able to keep other demands sufficiently at bay to accomplish even what I have.

Many individuals have provided intellectual stimulation to my thinking about this topic over the years, but I should especially like to mention Harald Atmanspacher, Richard Berengarten, Paul Bishop, Joseph Cambray, David Curtis, Edward Kelly, Jeffrey Kripal, Paul Marshall, and Robert Segal, as well as Maureen Doolan, Eleanor Peat, Shantena Sabbadini, and their colleagues at the Pari Center, who at various times all provided occasions or prompts for me to get my inner ruminations into external form. At the University of Essex, I have had valuable discussions with colleagues, above all David Henderson and Christian McMillan, as well as with my doctoral, master's, and undergraduate students on whom I have inflicted my thinking-in-progress over the years.

Some of the material in the book has been reworked from earlier publications and is used here with grateful acknowledgment: Parts of

Chapter 1 were previously published in "Mystical Experience and the Scope of C. G. Jung's Holism," in E. Kelly & P Marshall (Eds.), *Consciousness Unbound: Liberating Mind from the Tyranny of Materialism* (Lanham, MA: Rowman & Littlefield, 2021), pp. 139–174; parts of Chapter 2 in "Anomalous Phenomena, Synchronicity, and the Re-sacralization of the Modern World," in S. Kakar & J. Kripal (Eds.), *Seriously Strange: Thinking Anew About Psychic Experiences* (New Delhi: Penguin Viking, 2012) pp. 1-27, 275-283; parts of Chapter 3 in "Synchronicity and the Problem of Meaning in Science," in H. Atmanspacher & C. Fuchs (Eds.), *The Pauli–Jung Conjecture and Its Impact Today* (Exeter, UK: Imprint Academic, 2014) pp. 217–239; and parts of Chapter 4 in "Panentheism and the Undoing of Disenchantment," *Zygon: Journal of Religion and Science 52* (2017) pp. 1098–1122.

Finally, I should like to thank my wife, Shiho, and my children, Alasdair and Helen, for creating such a rich, loving, and enjoyable home environment as the necessary counterpoint to the solitude, and all too often the solipsism, of writing.

1

Disenchantment

In the autumn of 1917, as the First World War ground on in Europe, the Swiss psychiatrist Carl Gustav Jung (1875–1961) was at a critical juncture in his life. Four years previously, his period of intense and outwardly expansive engagement with Sigmund Freud (1856–1939) and the nascent psychoanalytic movement had come to an acrimonious end. Since then, partly prompted by concern for the psychological and social conditions that had given rise to the war (1963/1995, p. 200), he had been immersed in an experiment of self-exploration. This experiment involved entering imaginative and critical dialogue with personified contents of his unconscious mind, some emerging spontaneously, others deliberately evoked—the process dubbed in his memoirs as his "confrontation with the unconscious" (pp. 194–225). He had been recording and elaborating the results of this experiment in what became *The Red Book: Liber Novus* (2009/2012), the text of which was substantially completed by this time.[1] Within *The Red Book*, not destined to be published during his lifetime, were the seeds of the psychological model that would be unfolded in Jung's professional writings over the following 40 and more years. Indeed, Jung had begun to formulate elements of this model in papers on psychological types, the transcendent function, and the process of individuation (1913/1971b, 1916/1957/1969s, 1916/1977a). At the age of 42, he had just passed into what he would subsequently call "the second half of life" (1928/1996d, para. 114; 1930–1931/1969q, para. 777), when a person's interests typically shift from more biological to more cultural concerns. In his case, this transition was marked both inwardly by his encounter with the unconscious and his "refinding the soul" (2009/2012, pp.127–130) and

1

outwardly by the development of his distinctive model of complex or analytical psychology.

At around this same time, on 7 November 1917, the pioneering German social thinker Max Weber (1864–1920) delivered an invited lecture in Munich to a Bavarian student society (Radkau, 2005/2009, pp. 487–491). The lecture was titled "Science as a Vocation [*Wissenschaft als Beruf*]," and in it Weber (1919/1948d) gave classic expression to the now celebrated notion of "the disenchantment of the world [*Entzauberung der Welt*]" (p. 155)—a notion which, I shall argue, both illuminates the process Jung had been going through and, in turn, can be illuminated by the psychological model that emerged from Jung's process.

DISENCHANTMENT IN WEBER'S "SCIENCE AS A VOCATION"

Weber's lecture was an address to students who might be considering a scientific or academic career. He outlined the outer or material conditions of academic life, emphasizing the professional politics at work in universities, their increasing bureaucratization, and the large element of chance involved in getting onto a secure career track (1919/1948d, pp. 129–134). He also, at greater length, noted the inner conditions of academic life: the need not only for hard work and specialization, which might be within one's control, but also for passion, inspiration, gift or aptitude, and devotion to one's subject area, which are qualities whose presence is much more subject to chance again (pp. 134–156). Indeed, Weber summed up academic life as "a mad hazard" (p. 134). Nor, he argued, is it obvious what is the meaning of academic life. Whereas in the past knowledge was pursued in order to find the true reality of being, art, nature, God, or happiness, such goals, he stated, are no longer credible. Science and scholarship are now informed by the principle of progress, which implies that all their findings are of only temporary validity and are destined to be—indeed are intended to be—superseded (pp. 138–144).

Academic work can thus find no completeness within the span of a person's life, nor can it provide any answers to the fundamental question of how we should live. It cannot prove any value, not even the value of its own activity, for we live in a "polytheism" of competing and incompatible values, for none of which can there be any ultimate warrant (pp. 147–149). This, for Weber, makes it inappropriate for academics to assume authority based on their own experience or personality or to offer prophetic or political leadership in the classroom, for these accomplishments and approaches can have no justification in academic work as such (pp. 149–150). Rather than establishing ultimate values and goals, what academic work can legitimately and more modestly offer, Weber argued, are, first, the knowledge and methods individuals need in order to achieve whatever goals they do set themselves; second, salubrious encounters with facts that are "inconvenient" for those goals and that might therefore prompt enhanced self-reflection; and third, a requirement to clarify their actions by giving an account of their own ultimate standpoint or values (pp. 150–152).

Underpinning this description by Weber of scientific and academic life is his view that the modern world is characterized by "disenchantment." "Disenchantment" is the usual English translation of the German term *Entzauberung*, which more literally means "de-magification," or "loss of magic"; it is sometimes also translated as "elimination of magic." In previous ages, Weber relates, people used to believe in gods, spirits, and other mysterious forces that they could pray to and influence by "magical means" in order to acquire knowledge and achieve results in the world (p. 139). Over the course of the millennia, with "increasing intellectualization and rationalization" and eventually the development of science and technology, belief in these mysterious forces has become increasingly unnecessary and has waned. Although individual persons today might have no greater knowledge of the conditions in which they live than did those in earlier times, they have the belief, thanks to the empiricism and reason of science, that, if they wished to know or do something, it would be possible to know or do it by "technical means and calculations," without invoking any "mysterious incalculable forces" (p. 139). The disenchanted modern world for Weber is thus a world that has been stripped of genuine mystery.

However, there are for Weber important limits to what can be known by the empiricism and reason of science. Crucially, disenchanted modern science cannot obtain any knowledge of values or meaning. "Who," Weber asks rhetorically, "still believes that the findings of astronomy, biology, physics, or chemistry could teach us anything about the meaning of the world?" (p. 142) Indeed, he states, "these natural sciences ... are apt to make the belief that there is such a thing as the 'meaning' of the universe die out at its very roots" (p. 142). The sciences have their presuppositions about the value of obtaining knowledge of the natural world, but these presuppositions cannot be proved correct (pp. 143–144); "still less," Weber reiterates, "can it be proved that the existence of the world which these sciences describe is worth while, that it has any 'meaning,' or that it makes sense to live in such a world" (p. 144). Any attempt to make such valuations would interfere with the proper activity of science, for "whenever the man of science introduces his personal value judgment, a full understanding of the facts ceases" (p. 146). The disenchanted modern world for Weber is thus a world that lacks inherent meaning.

Not only is it impossible to derive values from facts, but it is also, for Weber, impossible to obtain knowledge of any spiritual, divine, or "metaphysical" realities deemed to be beyond the empirical world. Whereas in the past, knowledge was pursued in order to access higher realities—providing "the way to true being," "the way to true art," "the way to true nature," "the way to true God," "the way to true happiness" (p. 143)— modern science no longer considers it possible to know these "former illusions" (p. 143) or indeed to access any reality beyond the empirical world; presuppositions about such things "lie beyond the limits of 'science'" and "do not represent knowledge in the usual sense" (p. 154). The disenchanted modern world for Weber is thus unrelated to any spiritual, divine, or other metaphysical realities.

This combination of features of the disenchanted modern world—its being stripped of genuine mystery, lacking inherent meaning, and being unrelated to any spiritual or divine realities—has for Weber a further implication regarding how we are to understand the relationship between science and religion. Since the deliverances of science and reason provide no evidence for the putative transcendent realities and values of religion but can, alternatively, furnish credible naturalistic explanations of alleged religious phenomena (p. 147), one can, Weber argued, only make the step into religion by abandoning science and reason, making an "intellectual sacrifice" (p. 155). The disenchanted modern world for Weber is thus a world in which science and religion are irreconcilable.[2]

JUNG'S EXPERIENCE OF DISENCHANTMENT

With the notion of disenchantment, Weber articulated an important aspect, or set of aspects, of the European intellectual and cultural environment of his day. To many, then and now, his account has rung true, and it remains one of the most powerful narratives of modernity (Josephson-Storm, 2017, p. 4; Yelle & Trein, 2021). In the case of Jung, the narrative of disenchantment helps to clarify part of the context that led to his personal crisis, his writing of *The Red Book*, and his development of what we now know as analytical psychology.

Jung does not appear to have been more than casually aware of Weber, there is no evidence that he ever read "Science as a Vocation," and he never used the term "disenchantment" (*Entzauberung*) in his writing.[3] Nevertheless, he was clearly aware of and profoundly influenced by the condition or process described by Weber, which, though expressed in different terms, was a central preoccupation of his work from the beginning of his professional life until his death.

Already in his *Zofingia Lectures* (1896–1899/1983), delivered to his student fraternity between 1896 and 1899—about two decades before Weber's lecture to the Bavarian student society in Munich—Jung had grappled with the loss of mystery in contemporary rationalistic understandings of Christianity, with the separation of morality from science (that is, of values from facts), and with the materialistic denial of the existence and accessibility of spiritual reality (paras. 14–16, 135–142, 237–291). Prefiguring his later work, he not only noted these cultural developments but also sought ways to challenge them.

In much of his early psychiatric work, Jung gravitated toward phenomena that were either outright mysterious or at least resistant to rational understanding, including many that might be deemed "enchanted." However, so long as he was establishing himself professionally, he still tended to put the accent on understanding these phenomena scientifically. For instance, in his doctoral dissertation, "On the Psychology and Pathology of So-Called Occult Phenomena" (1902/1957), he investigated the world of spirit mediumship, reframing its "magical" or "occult" performances in scientific and medical terms. In his work at the Burghölzli mental hospital between 1900 and 1909, he similarly deployed scientific methods, including cutting-edge developments of word association and psychogalvanometric tests, to understand rationally the seemingly irrational world of madness (1973b). Through his involvement with Freud between 1906 and 1913, he acquired further techniques, such as dream and transference analysis, for making intelligible the unknown or unconscious dimensions of the mind, at the same time as he was exposed to Freud's own deeply rationalistic and reductive approach to knowledge (1961; 1963/1995, pp. 169–193).

In each of these early periods of work, Jung explored the extent to which seemingly mysterious psychic phenomena were susceptible to empirical and rational, that is, scientific, explanation. The results were impressive, and the prospects for the psychology of the unconscious as a science must have seemed bright. But Jung was clearly also deeply interested in what such rational approaches could not satisfactorily explain—experiences of mystery, meaning, and the sacred—and he felt that the failure to attend sufficiently to those recalcitrant areas of experience was cutting him off from important aspects of his being, from what he called his "soul" (2009/2012, p. 127). The pressure of this neglect seems to have accumulated and to have eventually precipitated the series of personal outer and inner events that resulted in his writing of the texts that would become his *Red Book*. The "overall theme" of this work is, in the words of its editor Sonu Shamdasani, "how Jung regains his soul and overcomes the contemporary malaise of spiritual alienation" (2009/2012, p. 48). Otherwise put, it is an attempt to address the condition of disenchantment to which Jung's own scientific work, for all its frequently "enchanted" subject matter, had been contributing.

In addition to his personal experience of disenchantment, Jung was undoubtedly also affected by observing such experiences in others. For example, in *Memories, Dreams, Reflections* (1963/1995), he describes the effect on him of his clergyman father's "religious doubts" and ultimate "religious collapse" in the face of the dominant materialism and rationalism of the times (pp. 110–115). And later, when illustrating his ideas with clinical material, he returned multiple times to cases, such as those now known to be of Maggie Reichstein (1894–1975) (de Moura, 2019) and Wolfgang Pauli (1900–58) (Gieser, 2019), in which the key factor appears to have been the analysands' excessive intellectuality that was cutting them off from a richer, more balanced, and more meaningful mode of being.

The condition or process of disenchantment continued to form part of the background of Jung's thought for the rest of his life. He may never have used the term "disenchantment," but in his Terry Lectures on "Psychology and Religion," delivered at Yale University in 1937, he referred in closely equivalent terms to "the historical process of world despiritualization" (1938/1940/1969n, para. 141). Again, in an interview with the historian of religions Mircea Eliade in 1952, he described the modern world as "desacralized" (McGuire & Hull, 1978, p. 230). Like Weber, Jung highlighted the excessively intellectual and rational character of modernity (1957/1970e, paras. 488–504). Also like Weber, Jung remarked specifically on the loss of genuine mystery, inherent meaning, and relationship to spiritual reality: "We have stripped all things of their mystery and numinosity," he declared; "nothing is holy any longer" (1961/1977q, para. 582). Enchantment had vanished quite literally, for "We have ceased to believe in magical formulas ... our world seems to be disinfected of ... superstitious numina" (para. 586). The establishment of facts undermined the security of values: "Through scientific understanding," he remarked, "our world has become dehumanized" (para. 585). Also diminished was belief in our being related to a reality beyond the empirical: "Life is too rational," Jung lamented, "there is no symbolic existence in which I am something else, in which I am fulfilling my role, my role as one of the actors in the divine drama of life" (1939/1977p, para. 628). The lack of such a symbolic, spiritual, or divine aspect, Jung felt, is why life is so often experienced as "awful, grinding, banal" (para. 627).

RESPONSES TO DISENCHANTMENT

Weber's narrative of disenchantment prompted at the time, and has continued to prompt, a variety of responses and evaluations. Weber himself (1919/1948d) was far from optimistic about the social and cultural consequences of the condition or process that he had delineated. Bound up as it was with increasing rationalization and intellectualization (p. 155), disenchantment, he believed, while freeing people from illusion and promoting extraordinary scientific and economic advances, would at the same time lead to an ever more thoroughly bureaucratized society (1922/1948a). He depicted the nature of such a society in a variety of bleak metaphors: It would encase individuals in its "iron cage" (1904–1905/2001, p. 123); turn each into "a single cog in an ever-moving mechanism" (1922/1948a, p. 228); and lead them relentlessly toward "a polar night of icy darkness and hardness" (1919/1948b, p. 128). The outcome of a millennia-long historical process (1919/1948d, p. 138), disenchantment has now become, Weber argued, "the fate of our times" (p. 155), a condition that we cannot credibly release ourselves from and therefore simply have to acknowledge, endure, and orientate ourselves within. In a similarly pessimistic spirit, the critical theorists Max Horkheimer and Theodor Adorno (1947/2002), reflecting on the emergence of totalitarianism in the first half of the 20th century, argued that the disenchantment or demythologization inherent in the European Enlightenment, with its relentless fostering of instrumental rationality, is itself a pernicious form of enchantment or mythology—one that ultimately leads to domination of nature, dehumanization, and, in their vivid phrase, an earth "radiant with triumphant calamity" (p. 1).

Others, such as the philosopher Hans Blumenberg (1983; Bennett, 2001, pp. 65–75) and the historian, philosopher, and sociologist Marcel Gauchet (1997), have shared the sense of the inevitability of disenchantment but have been more positive about its consequences. It is, indeed, possible to present a strong narrative highlighting many cultural benefits for which the process of disenchantment can take a major part of the credit, as less sanguine commentators also acknowledge (Berman, 1981; Tarnas, 1991/1996, 2006; Harrington, 1996; Taylor, 2007).

Disenchantment

In brief, the process of purging magic from our images of God and nature can be argued to have created space for the development of more theoretical, intellectual, rational modes of thought. Over time this has led to the emergence of science with its provision of empirical explanations, effective predictions, and the ability to manipulate and control the environment. This in turn has resulted in extraordinary advances in technology, agriculture, construction, manufacturing, transport, and communication, with vastly improved economic conditions for many, unprecedented availability of education and health care, and an overall enrichment of lifestyles.

Psychologically, the development of more theoretical modes of thought has given rise to forms of consciousness in which there is greater differentiation between self and others and between self and world, with a concomitant enhanced sense of self-determination and agency. Such forms of consciousness have been experienced as inwardly freer, and they have been accompanied by demands, often successful, for a corresponding external freedom from hierarchical social and political structures.

The assumptions of disenchantment on which the above narrative is based have for many been so "naturalized" (Taylor, 2007, p. 560) that they pass almost unquestioned. Indeed, some such view as the above could be considered the default position in most scientific, academic, and intellectual discourses from Weber's time to the present.

However, many even of the same thinkers who have acknowledged these benefits (Berman, 1981; Tarnas, 1991/1996, 2006; Harrington, 1996; Taylor, 2007) have also noted the more negative implications of disenchantment. They have observed, in sum, that the intellectualization and rationalization that are the concomitants of disenchantment have ended up being heavily one-sided, leading to an overall loss of the sense of the sacred and the objectively symbolic, of a cosmic order that can ground meaning and value. Ontologically, everything has become reducible to matter, which, for all that it may be "in motion," is considered to be fundamentally dead, with life and consciousness mere epiphenomena of its interactions.

Within a disenchanted perspective, rather than experience the world personally, participatively, dialogically, we experience it impersonally and atomistically, with a profound sense of division between ourselves and others, as well as between ourselves and nature. We understand the world, other people, and even ourselves as objects, to be explained mechanistically and deployed instrumentally for ends that have no ultimate or universally agreed grounding. At the individual level, such division and objectification create an existential sense of meaninglessness and self-alienation, often marked by anxiety, depression, and psychosis, along with attempts to escape these conditions through therapy or cultural and behavioral distractions. At social, political, and environmental levels, the objectification of others and nature leads to stifling bureaucratic organizations on the one hand and to exploitative and predatory relations on the other.

Even in Weber's day, there were thinkers who, with these kinds of implications in mind, did not, as Weber (1919/1948d) did, accept them as "the fate of our times" (p. 155) but challenged disenchantment. For example, in the life and mind sciences and even in the physical sciences during the first decades of the 20th century, there were major programs of work that developed forms of holism and vitalism to resist the perceived reductionist, mechanistic, and deterministic implications of disenchantment (Harrington, 1996; Asprem, 2014, pp. 100–198). Holism, in the form of the systems theory of Gregory Bateson (1904–80), was also pivotal in what was one of the most trenchant and influential later challenges to disenchantment, Morris Berman's *The Reenchantment of the World* (1981).[4]

Proposals for resisting disenchantment—now often explicitly framed as attempts to "reenchant" and often with a holistic emphasis—have continued to appear up to the present (Griffin, 1988; Flannagan, 1996; Tarnas, 2006, pp. 16–25, 50–60; Crawford, 2020; Meijer & De Vriese, 2021). In some cases, these attempts have been framed in secular rather than sacred terms. For it has been noted that "each time religion reluctantly withdrew from a particular area of experience [i.e., whenever disenchantment occurred], a new, thoroughly secular strategy for reenchantment cheerfully emerged to fill the void" (Landy & Saler, 2009, p. 1).[5]

There have also been attempts to qualify the narrative of disenchantment by showing that disenchantment has been far from complete or ubiquitous and that significant possibilities of enchantment have always remained at the heart of modern culture, both élite and popular (Bennett, 2001; Partridge, 2004; Sherry, 2009; Curry, 2019). As Egil Asprem (2014, pp. 38–40) has pointed out, the notion of disenchantment is, to use another of Weber's (1922/2019) terms, "ideal-typical" (pp. 81–82), which is to say that it represents a condition that people would be in if they were fully rational. Since people are not fully rational, it would not be surprising, from a Weberian perspective, that in many, perhaps most, actual cases, individuals have been only partially disenchanted. For example, scientists and other thinkers who have in principle adhered to a disenchanted view have nevertheless engaged in efforts to reconcile their science with religion through various forms of natural theology (Asprem, 2014, pp. 198–286) or have happily derived values from facts when, for instance, justifying forms of social organization with appeals to evolutionary science (pp. 60–61). Perhaps most surprising of all, as Jason Josephson-Storm (2017) shows, is that even many of the social-scientific theorists whose work promoted disenchantment remained curiously engaged with forms of enchanted thought, such as spiritualism, psychical research, esotericism, and mysticism: James Frazer (1954–1941), Edward Tylor (1832–1917), Freud, Adorno (1903–69), Rudolf Carnap (1891–1970), and, as we shall discuss more fully later, Weber himself are among the unlikely figures who can be shown to have had such involvements.

JUNG'S RESPONSE TO DISENCHANTMENT

In the remainder of this chapter, I shall argue that Jung's psychological model, in particular its core process of individuation, can be understood as a particularly rich response to disenchantment. On the one hand, it repudiates each of disenchantment's implicit epistemological assumptions about the validity of mystery, meaning, and spiritual reality, and as such, can be considered a forthright form of reenchantment. Yet, within its wider process, individuation also acknowledges both the perpetual need for disenchantment and the continuing presence of naïve enchantment. From this encompassing perspective, Jung's model arguably also helps to make sense of the complexity and ambivalence of other prior responses to disenchantment.

The richness, complexity, and controversial nature of Jung's response to disenchantment is reflected in the variety of previous discussions of his work in relation to the notion. Berman (1981, pp. 78–88), for example, writing as a historian and social critic, invokes Jung's psychology, alongside the work of Bateson and Wilhelm Reich (1897–1957), as part of his attempt to articulate a new holistic metaphysics that will address the problem of disenchantment at its roots. Berman examines Jung's use of alchemy as a form of thought that has not suffered from the Cartesian split between mind and matter and hence has remained "participative," though he also considers Jung's return to the past to be by itself inadequate for addressing problems in the present.

Another appeal to Jung's psychology that highlights its value for fostering participative thought as a means of addressing disenchantment occurs in the cultural historian Richard Tarnas's *Cosmos and Psyche* (2006, pp. 16–25, 50–60). Tarnas picks up on the importance of Jung's concept of synchronicity for this purpose. Asprem, in his *The Problem of Disenchantment* (2014, pp. 144–147), also focuses on synchronicity, especially Jung's collaboration with Pauli on the topic, as an example of how a new esoteric concept could be born from "engagements with the problem of disenchantment from inside of dominant scientific discourses of the early twentieth century" (p. 103).

A work that has clearly drawn on resources of Jung's thought, even though Jung's theory is not discussed explicitly, is Thomas Moore's *The Re-enchantment of Everyday Life* (1996). Aimed at a more popular than scholarly or clinical readership, Moore's book proposes strategies for rediscovering enchantment in life across a wide range of areas. In doing so, he shows himself vividly aware of the embarrassment one can feel in promoting such perspectives in a predominantly secular culture.

More recently, there have been several explicit studies of Jung's relationship to disenchantment by clinicians and scholars explicitly aligned with his work. Among analysts, Wolfgang Giegerich (2012), in a provocative critical reading of Jung's psychology, argues that the enchanting elements to be found in it are regressive, evidence of what Giegerich calls a "disenchantment complex," a failure on Jung's part fully to undergo "the initiation into his personal adulthood (in a *psychological* sense) and at the same time into modernity" (p. 17). Giegerich notes the "equiprimordiality" of enchantment and disenchantment and logical priority of disenchantment, observing that it is only with the concept of disenchantment that the concept of enchantment comes into being at all (pp. 9–11). Michael Whan (2012), focusing on the connection between myth and place, similarly prioritizes disenchantment, which he sees as "the soul's work: the dialectical labor of negation and self-relation: namely, an alchemical *opus contra naturam*" (p. 34).

Contrastingly, Mark Saban (2012) also considers that enchantment and disenchantment coexist in Jung's work, but he takes a much more positive view of the doubleness. For Saban, the enchanting and disenchanting aspects of Jung's thought reflect his "Number 1" and "Number 2" personalities, both aspects are necessary, and the "antinomial" tension between them is precisely what makes Jung's psychology modern.

A more uncompromisingly critical view of disenchantment is offered by Andrew Fellows in his book *Gaia, Psyche, and Deep Ecology: Navigating Climate Change in the Anthropocene* (2019). He relates the current ecological crisis to the hegemony of the disenchanted worldview (pp. 68–70) and, in an approach consonant with that of the present book, deploys analytical psychology, especially the process of individuation, to propose strategies for addressing its perilous impacts.

Among academics, the literary scholar Terence Dawson (2012) demonstrates with reference to E. T. A Hoffman's tale "The Sandman" the value of Jung's concepts of the archetype and archetypal image for understanding the nature of enchantment and its hidden perils of possession. And the Germanist Paul Bishop (2012), discussing the psychological dynamics of disenchantment at the core of the crisis afflicting modern universities, aptly notes that "analytical psychology itself is a symptom of (as well as a reaction, a response, and indeed a solution to) the disenchantment of the modern world" (p. 59).

My own prior work on Jung and disenchantment, like Saban's, has noted the antinomial nature of Jung's thought (Main, 2011, 2013a, 2013b, 2015) and, like Tarnas's, has presented reenchantment as a substantive stage or state associated with nondualistic (participative and unitive) forms of consciousness (Main, 2014, pp. 232–237; 2021b, pp. 148–159). My main emphasis has been the pivotal role of synchronicity for reenchantment (2011, 2013b, 2014), as well as the need to ground a reenchanted perspective in a different—specifically, I suggest, a panentheistic—form of metaphysics (2017, 2021a, 2021b). These are all issues that I develop in the present work, whose emphasis, in line with Bishop's formulation, is that analytical psychology, and in particular its core process of individuation, is both a response and an intended solution to disenchantment.

INDIVIDUATION

As we have seen, even before he began to formulate the concept of individuation, Jung's psychological thinking was clearly addressing issues relevant to the problem of disenchantment. He explored, rather than explained away, the unconscious and its "mysterious incalculable forces," including what he called complexes and later archetypes (1973b). He highlighted the importance of fantasy thinking and imagination as a complement to directed thinking with its fostering of intellectualization and rationalization (1911–1912/1952/1967, paras. 4–46). He drew attention to the functions of feeling and intuition, which could establish values and meanings, in addition to the functions of thinking and sensation, which mainly established facts (1913/1971b). And he invoked final, not only causal, forms of explanation (1916/1966e, para. 501n19).

With the concept of individuation, all these emphases and tendencies in Jung's thought were subsumed into a coherent, if complex, overall process. In brief, individuation is the developmental process of becoming a unique self through the ongoing synthesis of consciousness and the unconscious. Jung articulated the process in a variety of ways, of which the following is a summary (based mainly on Jung, 1928/1996d and 1951/1968b, paras. 1–67).

For Jung, psychological development begins in childhood and early adulthood by one's developing and strengthening an ego to deal with the forces that assail one from the psychic world within and the social world without. Such an ego is inevitably one-sided, having been forced by the pressures of its inner and outer environments to develop and thereby make conscious some psychic potentialities at the expense of others, which remain unconscious.

In Jung's understanding, however, the unconscious has an innate drive toward expressing itself as a whole. An opposition is therefore set up between consciousness, centered on the ego, and the unconscious. From the unconscious, contents emerge spontaneously—for example, in the form of dreams, fantasies, symptoms, and acausal convergences of events—to compensate and regulate consciousness in the interests of greater overall realization of the unconscious.

This process of encounter between the ego and the unconscious, which can be facilitated by psychotherapy and the deployment of techniques such as dream interpretation, transference analysis, and active imagination, is marked by the appearance of certain typical themes or problems, which demand to be integrated and made conscious. Such typical themes, problems, or "archetypes" needing to be encountered and integrated with the ego include above all the disavowed, often dark, side of one's personality (the "shadow") and the contrasexual element of one's personality (the "anima" or "animus").

When a sufficient level of integration has been achieved between ego-consciousness and these archetypes, there can emerge a new center of the psyche, a center no longer only of consciousness, as was the ego, but of both consciousness and the unconscious. This new center is what Jung called the "self." The self is potentially there from the beginning as a kind of unconscious wholeness, but the aim of individuation is to realize it consciously. This is an extremely arduous, lifelong task, and it is full of pitfalls, not least the dangers of either the ego's becoming excessively assimilated by the self or the self's becoming excessively assimilated by the ego, both of which would result in pathological conditions, such as psychosis or inflation. "Conscious wholeness," Jung wrote more favorably, "consists in a successful union of ego and self, so that both preserve their intrinsic qualities" (1947/1954/1969g, para. 430n128).

This overall process of individuation corresponds, I suggest, with the process of transformation from an enchanted state to a disenchanted state to a reenchanted state, with the reenchanted state being for Jung the overarching and decisive one. The correspondence can be shown by highlighting some aspects of the typical developmental stages within the process of individuation outlined above. For this purpose, I present two further, differently inflected summaries of individuation. The first is based on an account (Stein, 2006) aimed at tracking the typical stages in which the individuation process is encountered during psychotherapy. For convenience, I shall refer to this as the psychotherapeutic model. Whereas Jung generally emphasized two halves of life (1930–1931/1969q), this first additional summary subdivides the first "half" into two stages, producing a three-stage model. The second additional summary, presented in more detail, is based on Jung's last extensive discussion of individuation, in *Mysterium Coniunctionis* (1955–1956/1970a), wherein he articulates the process in terms borrowed from alchemy. For convenience, I shall refer to this as the alchemical model. This model also recognizes three stages, though here the three stages all seem to be concerned with the second half of life. I shall return to these differences later.

One further point to note before exploring the possible correspondences between individuation and enchantment, disenchantment, and reenchantment is that the Jungian framing of the narrative of disenchantment is a psychological extrapolation from phenomena that have, since Weber, predominantly been discussed sociologically. What is being proposed here is that this Jungian psychological perspective, in addition to any therapeutic value it may have, may also yield insights that are reciprocally illuminating for sociological or psychosocial analyses. This would be entirely in keeping with Jung's own perception of his psychology as being inherently collective as well as individual. In his later work, Jung made this point repeatedly and in relation to several of his signature concepts: "the peculiar nature of the self," he wrote, "embraces the individual as well as society" (1958/1970b, para. 660); "the collective unconscious is anything but an incapsulated personal system; it is sheer objectivity, as wide as the world and open to all the world" (1934/1954/1968a, para. 46); and "Individuation does not shut one out from the world, but gathers the world to oneself" (1947/1954/1969g, para. 432). This entails for Jung the inseparability of social and psychological phenomena: "When a patient comes to us with a neurosis," he wrote, "he does not bring a part but the whole of his psyche, and with it the fragment of world on which that psyche depends, and without which it can never be properly understood" (1945/1996c, para. 212). How, then, with this psychosocial inflection in mind, might Jung's psychological model of individuation correspond to the narrative of disenchantment?

Three Stages of Individuation

Jung's model of individuation posits an initial undifferentiated and unconscious state, a preconscious fusion of subjectivity with the world. Drawing on the work of Erich Neumann (1954, 1955), Murray Stein (2006) describes this initial stage as the "maternal" or "containment/nurturance" stage of individuation (pp. 199, 200–204). Jung considers this to be the state of mind of so-called "primitive" peoples and of children. This state, for which Jung also borrows Lucien Lévy-Bruhl's (1857–1939) term "participation mystique," broadly corresponds, I suggest, with the state of enchantment. It is a state characterized by identification, in which all aspects of the world seem animated and to behave according to the influence of magical forces.

With the development of ego-consciousness, there emerges increasing differentiation between self and world, subject and object. Greater critical capacities arise, including eventually the ability to notice and begin to withdraw projections. In Stein's terms, this is the "paternal" or "adapting/adjusting" stage of individuation (2006, pp. 199, 204–209). Jung considers this to be the state of mind of young adults who are coming to terms with life's realities and acquiring independence. It broadly corresponds, I suggest, with the state of disenchantment, experienced as freedom from former animistic delusions, in which the world is now seen as regulated impersonally by natural laws and hence as indifferent to human wishes.

The final, "individual" or "centering/integrating" stage of individuation (pp. 199, 209–212) is, according to Stein, "usually entered with a rather depressed and questioning attitude" (p. 210)—an attitude that can readily be seen to correspond with a state of disenchantment now experienced not as freedom from delusions but as deanimation. In this stage, writes Stein, "There is a shift in interest and emphasis towards reaching out to dimensions of living that have less to do with survival and more to do with meaning. Spiritual life becomes more crucially important and individualized" (p. 210). It is at this stage that the main work of integrating the opposites takes place (p. 212). A person comes to be centered less in the ego and more in the self, and as a result "feels less alienated from all of humanity and from the profound complexities of reality" (p. 212). The references here to dimensions of meaning, the importance of spiritual life, and the overcoming of alienation suggest that this stage corresponds with the state of reenchantment.

Stein emphasizes the two major transitions between these stages— from the maternal to the paternal and from the paternal to the individual. These would be phases where in the first case disenchantment and in the second case reenchantment appear not so much as states but as processes. Josephson-Storm (2017) has suggested that the term "Entzauberung" might be more aptly translated as "disenchanting" than as "disenchantment" (p. 300), and similarly "reenchanting" might be a more appropriate term than "reenchantment." But whether focusing on the three states of enchantment, disenchantment, and reenchantment or on the two processes of transition from enchantment to disenchantment and from disenchantment to reenchantment, the overall correspondence of the stages of individuation with these states or processes is compelling.

In presenting the three-stage model, Stein (2006) observes that, "Generally synchronicity ... plays an important role in the entry into and in the ongoing process of individuation in the third stage" (p. 210). On one level, this statement means simply that synchronistic events—meaningful coincidences—tend to occur at this stage of individuation. But on another level, the statement draws attention to the radical implications of synchronicity for the transformation of consciousness, which constitute an important part of what is taking place in both late-stage individuation and, I would argue, reenchantment. Both these levels will prove important in subsequent chapters where the role of synchronicity in reenchantment is discussed in detail.

Individuation and Alchemy

Jung believed that he had found a premodern parallel to the process of individuation in the symbolism of medieval alchemy, and he elaborated this parallel over the final three decades of his life in a series of studies of the relationship between psychological and alchemical phenomena and concepts. He explained this work as being necessary because the partial nature of all clinical case studies of individuation meant that it was impossible to arrive at a picture of the whole process of individuation from those case studies alone. The symbolism of alchemy, by contrast, was much richer, having been built up over many centuries by numerous practitioners. Taken as a whole, the alchemical tradition provided Jung with "sufficient room," he wrote, "to describe the individuation process at least in its essential aspects" (1955–1956/1970a, para. 792). At the end of his final major study of alchemy, *Mysterium Coniunctionis* (1955–1956/ 1970a), Jung encapsulated the process in terms provided by the 16th-century alchemist Gerhard Dorn (ca. 1530–1584). In summarizing the process below, I shall again note connections to the framing of individuation as a process of enchantment, disenchantment, and re-enchantment.

Because of Jung's use of alchemical terminology, this account of individuation is difficult to present concisely, but there are nevertheless important reasons for attempting to come to terms with it here. Above all, the account draws on Jung's last major exposition of individuation, which he himself considered to be the culmination of his work (1963/1995, p. 248). Moreover, the account focuses on the late stages of individuation, which are particularly relevant for understanding the pivotal process of reenchantment. Again, Jung's expressing his ideas within the framework and symbolism of alchemy is significant from a historical point of view in that alchemy mostly dates from a time preceding the rapid acceleration of the process of disenchantment from the time of the Scientific Revolution and Enlightenment and is part of a worldview in which magic also still figured prominently (Berman, 1981; Hanegraaff, 2012). Finally, in this account, as we shall see, Jung not only provides more detail but also takes his thought further than he does elsewhere—to a point, indeed, that will prove crucial in reconsidering the relationship between Jung and Weber at the end of the chapter.

Dorn described the alchemical process as involving a series of three conjunctions. The first conjunction, which he called the *unio mentalis* ("mental union"), consists of a union of spirit and soul (Jung, 1955–1956/1970a, paras. 664–676). Dorn considered that in the natural human state there was "an inextricable interweaving of the soul with the body, which together formed a dark unity (the *unio naturalis* [natural union])," variously referred to by the alchemists as "the *nigredo* [blackness], the chaos, the *massa confusa* [confused mass]" (para. 696). Jung describes it as "The original, half-animal state of unconsciousness" (para. 696). However, through the operation of spirit—that is, through the discriminating power of "conscious and rational insight"—it is possible to extract the soul from its "enchainment" to the body, to free it from "its fetters in the things of sense," and thus "to set up a rational, spiritual-psychic position over against the turbulence of the emotions," a position "immune to the influences of the body" (para. 696). In Jung's psychological and psychotherapeutic terms, this "overcoming of the body" involves "making conscious and dissolving the projections that falsify the patient's view of the world and impede his self-knowledge" (paras. 696, 673). Acquiring greater self-knowledge (paras. 674, 711) brings neurotic symptoms "under the control of consciousness" and fosters "inner certainty" and "self-reliance" (para. 756).

This first conjunction can be understood as depicting the transition from a state of enchantment to a state of disenchantment. The state of enchantment is the unconscious identity or fusion ("*participation mystique*") between the psyche and the body and between the self and the world. The state of disenchantment is the differentiation, discrimination, or separation of the psyche from the body and of the self from the world with the aid of the spiritual intellect and its "conscious and rational insight." Becoming free of "the turbulence of the emotions," "the influences of the body," and "the projections that falsify [one's] view of the world and impede [one's] self-knowledge" and thereby bringing neurotic symptoms under the control of consciousness and fostering "inner certainty" and "self-reliance" are clearly major psychological and spiritual achievements. But these qualities and the discriminating, dualistic consciousness on which they are based come at a cost. Such "mental union [*unio mentalis*]" is, Jung notes, "purely intrapsychic" (para. 664); it is a state of "interior oneness" (para. 670). As such, it leaves the body and the material world unintegrated. Indeed, as Jung elaborates, it results in a deep split of the unified spirit and soul from matter and the body (para. 664). Jung does not for this reason denigrate the process, which he considers "indispensable for the differentiation of consciousness" (para. 672). However, since it was the soul that animated the body, a consequence of the soul's separation from the body by its union with spirit is that "the body and its world" appear "dead" (para. 742)—part of the very condition of disenchantment. The problem confronting the alchemists who reached this stage was how to reanimate the body by reuniting it with the soul in a way that was not simply a return to the confusion of the natural union (*unio naturalis*) (para. 742). This was the task of Dorn's second conjunction.

In Dorn's terms, the solution to the problem of how to reunite the *unio mentalis* with the body was the alchemical process resulting in production of the *caelum*, the "heaven," "the kingdom of heaven on earth," "a heavenly substance in the body," the "blue quintessence" (paras. 691–963, 703–706, 757–758, 764). Dorn described various alchemical procedures to produce this mysterious process and substance (paras. 681–685), but in Jung's interpretation such procedures are projected, symbolic expressions of the process of individuation and its facilitating method of active imagination (paras. 705–706). The *caelum* itself, the product of the process, is a symbol of the self. As such, the *caelum* was the *imago Dei*, the image of God, which could also be symbolized by the mandala (paras. 716–719, 757) and by the central alchemical figure of Mercurius, who, as both "matter and spirit," expressed for Jung that the self "embraces the bodily sphere as well as the psychic" (para. 717) and indeed represents not only a "spiritualization" of matter but also a "materialization of the spirit" (para. 764).

This second conjunction encapsulates the transition from a state of disenchantment to a state of reenchantment. The dualistic state in which consciousness appears to be separate from the world, psyche from matter, self from other, comes to be replaced by a more participative form of consciousness, in which this sense of separation begins to be dissolved. The world that seemed external, material, and other comes to be experienced as continuous with a wider sense of self. As a result, the world that had seemed to be inert and meaningless begins to show signs of animation, subjectivity, and participative relationship. Rather than being just material to be manipulated instrumentally for one's own ends, the world begins to make normative calls on one. From having been an "It," the world becomes a "Thou." The demands made by the world include that "the insights gained [in the second conjunction] should be made real," thereby "making a reality of the man who has acquired some knowledge of his paradoxical wholeness" (para. 679). The difficulty of effecting this transition from disenchanted to reenchanted consciousness cannot be overstated. It includes the work of integrating the anima/animus and of bringing about their union in the syzygy (cf. 1951/1968b, paras. 20–42; 1946/1966). The greater sense of unity toward which this process leads is experience of the self.

Again, however, this is not the conclusion of the process. What the second conjunction achieved was "the representation of the self in actual and visible form"—through symbolic images—but this, for Dorn and for Jung (1955–1956/1970a), was "a mere *rite d'entreé*, as it were a propaedeutic action and mere anticipation of [the self's] realization" (para. 759). The final realization, "a consummation of the *mysterium coniunctionis*," could be expected "only when the unity of spirit, soul, and body [i.e., the self or "whole man" (para. 760)] [was] made one with the original *unus mundus* ['one world']" (para. 664). This was Dorn's "third and highest degree of conjunction" (para. 760).

The concept of the *unus mundus* refers to "the potential world of the first day of creation, when nothing was yet 'in actu,' i.e., divided into two and many, but was still one" (para. 760); it is the *mundus archetypus*, the "archetypal world" (para. 761). Jung was clear that the state of being united with the *unus mundus*, made one with the "one world," is not a case of "a fusion of the individual with his environment, or even his adaptation to it, but a *unio mystica* with the potential world" (para. 767). He emphasized that this potential world "is not the world of sense" (para. 767) but the "background of our empirical world," the "transcendental psychophysical background" in which the conditions of empirical physical and psychical phenomena inhere (para. 769), "the eternal Ground of all empirical being" (para. 760).

As we have seen, reenchantment broadly corresponds with the stage of individuation that maps onto the second conjunction. What the third conjunction additionally does, theoretically at least, is to ground the process of reenchantment in an experience of unity with the creative ground of reality. On the one hand, participative consciousness is thus consolidated and taken further through an experience of unitive consciousness. The "It" which became a "Thou" is now realized as an "I," as *the* "I." On the other hand, the unity of the self with the creative ground of reality means that creativity out of the *unio mystica* can create entirely new states of reality, which when they first emerge unprocessed would also be experienced as new states of enchantment. The creative emergence of these new enchanted states can thus recursively trigger further potential processes of disenchantment, reenchantment, and mystical union.

As with the previously summarized psychotherapeutic model, so this alchemical model of individuation ascribes an important role to synchronicity. Jung (1955–1956/1970a) noted that, in Dorn's model, the alchemists who "solved the problem of realizing the *unio mentalis*, of effecting its union with the body, [and] thereby completed the second conjunction ... felt it as a magically effective action which ... imparted magical qualities" (para. 758). While these magical qualities may primarily have been "an inner effect," that is, a "psychological reaction to the formation of images," Jung, based on his psychological experience, "reserves judgement in regard to possible objective effects [i.e., synchronicities]" (para. 758 and note 227). He also suggested that, just as mandala symbols can give one a psychological intimation or experience of the *unus mundus*, so synchronicities can give one a parapsychological intimation or experience of it (para. 662). Indeed, he highlighted the ability of synchronicity to reveal "the universal interrelationship of events," "the unity of the world," "an inter-connection or unity of causally unrelated events," and the "unitary aspect of being which can very well be described as the *unus mundus*" (para. 662). With these formulations, Jung seems to be suggesting that synchronicity can even propel one toward the third conjunction, "when the unity of spirit, soul, and body is made one with the original *unus mundus*" (para. 664).

BREAKING THE SPELL OF DISENCHANTMENT: THE COUNTERMAGIC OF INDIVIDUATION

In the psychotherapeutic model of individuation, the three stages with which enchantment, disenchantment, and reenchantment have been correlated span the whole of biological life, from birth to late maturity. In the alchemical model of individuation, by contrast, the three conjunctions all seem to occur within late maturity and to be phases of consciously undertaken work of psychological and spiritual transformation, represented only by the third stage in the psychotherapeutic model. Moreover, disenchantment correlates with the first conjunction and reenchantment with the second conjunction in the alchemical model, whereas these correlations are with the second and third (or at least the transitions to the second and third) stages in the psychotherapeutic model. Finally, the third conjunction in the alchemical model is not explicated in the psychotherapeutic model.[6]

These differences reflect Jung's predominant focus, especially in his alchemical work, on the second half of life and late-stage individuation. The alchemical model provides, as it were, a more focused look at the stage in which Jung is most interested, where individuation is taken up as a consciously abetted rather than just naturally unfolding process. Within this more focused perspective, the correlations with enchantment, disenchantment, and reenchantment, despite the noted differences, remain apt. In both models, the process of transformation proceeds from an enchanted to a disenchanted to a reenchanted state, such that, crucially, disenchantment supersedes naïve enchantment but is not the culminating state. The culminating state is reenchantment, and the alchemical model, as presented in *Mysterium Coniunctionis*, presents Jung's most advanced account of its reach.[7]

Considering Jung's predominant interest in its late stage, the process of individuation is sometimes wholly identified with that stage (1939/1968f, para. 489), the earlier stages in the psychotherapeutic model being associated rather with processes of adaptation and integration (Samuels et al., 1986, p. 76). From the perspective of its goal, individuation can be said to be primarily concerned with reenchantment. To clarify the sense in which individuation may indeed reenchant, we can briefly revisit the theoretical implications of disenchantment—that there is no genuine mystery, inherent meaning, or relationship to spiritual or divine reality, and that science and religion are irreconcilable—and show how, at a general level, individuation challenges them, breaking their spell with its own deeper magic, as it were.

First, disenchantment implies that there is no genuine mystery. Contrary to this, individuation, especially in its later stages involves acknowledging and relating to factors—the collective unconscious and its archetypes—that precisely are "mysterious incalculable forces" influencing human behavior as well as events beyond the sphere of human behavior (1928/1996d, paras. 266–406). Not only, for Jung, are intrapsychic archetypal events, such as dreams and visions, genuinely creative and hence irreducible to any set of psychological, social, or cultural determinants (1947/1954/1969g, para. 417; 1961/1977q, paras. 521–559). There can also be, for Jung, even more mysterious, externally occurring events of an archetypal nature that acausally coincide with psychic events—that is, synchronicities (1952/1969r, paras. 841, 843–846). Moreover, the process of individuation culminates in realization of a factor, the self, that as a paradoxical coincidence of opposites (1951/1968b, para. 423) is quintessentially mysterious, especially if one further realizes its

25

union with the one world, or *unus mundus*, in the experience of mystical union (*unio mystica*) (1955–1956/1970a, para. 771).

Second, disenchantment implies that there is no inherent meaning in the world. Contrary to this, individuation for Jung presupposes a finality, purposiveness, and meaningfulness in the process of human development (1928/1996d, paras. 266–269, 405). He characterizes the archetypes that give structure to the process of individuation as each providing a "core of meaning" to a multiplicity of possible representations or experiences (1940/1968h, para. 266; 1947/1954/1969g, para. 417). He even describes the central archetype of the self, which guides individuation and is realized at its culmination, as "the archetype of orientation and meaning" (1963/1995, p. 224). In his essay "Synchronicity: An Acausal Connecting Principle" (1952/1969r), he makes clear that the kind of meaning he has in mind in discussing the archetypes that govern individuation is not just a subjective meaning projected onto external objects and events that in themselves are meaningless. He devotes a whole chapter, "Forerunners of the Idea of Synchronicity," to providing historical and cross-cultural support for the proposition that the archetypal meaning expressed by synchronicities is "objective" or "transcendental" (paras. 916–946).

Third, disenchantment implies that there can be no relationship to spiritual or divine reality. Contrary to this, individuation for Jung fosters relationship to numinous—spiritual—archetypes. More specifically, the process of individuation leads to realization of the archetype of the self, experience of which, Jung (1928/1996d) claims, is indistinguishable from experience of the God-image and as such represents "God within us" (para. 399). In Jung's understanding, individuation is precisely a religious process, whether he has in mind Western or Eastern forms of religion (1942/1954/1969t, paras. 414–448; 1939/1969d, paras. 906–907). As he asserted with emphasis, "*Individuation is the life in God*" (1956–1957/1977h para. 1624).

Finally, disenchantment implies that science and religion are irreconcilable, that in order to possess religion it is necessary to make an "intellectual sacrifice." Contrary to this, individuation for Jung is a process that is both religious, in the ways just described, and yet also scientific since, as he continually emphasized (1934/1950/1969i; 1973a, p. 529; 1976, pp. 294, 342), it is based on empirical observation of processes occurring in the psyche (see also Main, 2013c).[8]

ENCHANTMENT–DISENCHANTMENT–REENCHANTMENT

Although Jung himself usually focused on the final stage of individuation, the wider approach of viewing individuation as the entire process of human psychological development remains helpful for making sense of the complexity and ambivalence of other prior responses to disenchantment, such as the ones noted above in the sections "Responses to Disenchantment" and "Jung's Response to Disenchantment." Before reconsidering some of these responses, I shall briefly summarize the viewpoint I have extrapolated from Jung, namely, that *the process of individuation, though predominantly a form of reenchantment, can also be seen as a recursive process of enchantment, disenchantment, and reenchantment.*

In individuation, so this viewpoint goes, there is initially an enchanted state of unconscious identity between subject and object. In this enchanted state, the object appears animated because of its non-differentiation from the subject.

With increasing awareness, this enchanted state can transform into a disenchanted state of differentiated or dualistic consciousness in which the subject is experienced as essentially separate from the object. In this disenchanted state, the object appears unanimated, "dead," because of its essential separation from the subject.

Next, with yet a further increase of awareness, the disenchanted state can transform into a reenchanted state of participatory consciousness in which the subject and object are realized to be intrinsically related and indeed inseparable; both are parts of a larger whole or unity. In this reenchanted state, the object again appears animated, but this time in relation to a subject that remains fully conscious and discriminating.[9]

Finally, with fuller awareness again, the reenchanted state can transform into a mystical state of unitive consciousness in which subject and object become indistinguishable. It is not possible adequately to describe this mystical state in language, since language depends on distinguishing subject and object, but one approximation would be to say that it is a state of spontaneous creativity.

In describing the process of these transformations as recursive, what is meant is that the new realities emerging from the creativity of the *unio mystica* would in the first instance likely be experienced in the natural state of unconscious identity so that the whole process of differentiation, reintegration, and unity would need to be repeated in relation to these new realities.

One last point worth noting is that different aspects of a person or a culture might get drawn into the process of individuation at different times. This means that, in different respects, a person or culture could at any moment simultaneously exhibit characteristics of enchantment, disenchantment, and reenchantment. At neither the personal nor the cultural level does the lack of completeness or uniformity of enchantment, disenchantment, or reenchantment mean that one of those states or processes is definitively absent or cannot be predominant.

Some Jungian Perspectives on the Narrative of Disenchantment

Overall, as we have seen, Jung can be aligned with those who have criticized the condition of disenchantment and have promoted reenchantment as urgently needed in the present cultural moment. It is, for instance, no accident that some of the most notable attempts at reenchantment have been forms of holism (Berman, 1981; Harrington, 1996; Asprem, 2014, pp. 157–161), and Jung's reenchanting process of individuation is also profoundly holistic, aiming as it does at realization of the self, the "archetype of wholeness" (1951/1968b, para. 351; 1952/1969a, para. 757; 1955–1956/1970a, para. 777; see also Smith, 1990; Kelly, 1993; Main, 2019; McMillan et al., 2020; Main et al., 2021).

But while Jung criticized disenchantment and promoted reenchantment, he did not outright reject disenchantment or the rationalism with which it is associated. He recognized the perpetual need for the critical consciousness of disenchantment not only for its own undeniable, albeit ambivalent, benefits (1928/1931/1970d, para. 155; 1945/1977j, para. 1367) but also, more especially, to realize reenchantment. In terms of what I have been calling the psychotherapeutic model, one needs to undergo the disciplining and disenchanting stage of adapting to life's realities before one can effectively enter the centering and reenchanting stage of more fully realizing one's individuality (1921/1971a, para. 760). Similarly, in terms of what I have been calling the alchemical model, one needs to achieve the disenchanting state of the *unio mentalis* (separation of the mind from the body through its union with spirit) before one can achieve the reenchanting state of the *caelum* (reunion of the united mind-spirit with the body and its world) (1955–1956/1970a, paras. 669–680).

Where problems might arise is when disenchantment is identified with as the highest achievable state—when one is, as it were, under the spell of disenchantment, or, as Jung put it, when "we remain dominated by the great *Déesse Raison* [Goddess Reason], who is our overwhelming illusion" (1961/1977q, para. 598). This might easily occur because disenchantment, vis-à-vis the unconscious identifications of naïve enchantment, can be a liberatory and empowering state, associated, as we have seen, with a range of scientific, technological, organizational, and psychological attainments highly valued by the dominant global cultures. Moreover—to add a consideration from the Jungian perspective—as part of the archetypal process of individuation, the "subprocess" of disenchantment will have its own measure of archetypal fascination.

Another factor enhancing the attractiveness of disenchantment is the unconvincingness of much of what is proffered as reenchantment. Strategies for fostering belief in mystery, meaningfulness, and spiritual reality, which abound in popular literature,[10] often seem inauthentic, escapist, and, if they were pursued, likely ineffectual. In many cases, they seem more like regressions to naïve enchantment than attempts to undertake the arduous work of finding a way *beyond* disenchantment. Weber himself (1919/1948d), without using the word "reenchantment," was scathing about those "modern intellectuals" who, in an attempt to reacquire some of the mystique of religion, "play at decorating a sort of domestic chapel with small sacred images from all over the world, or they produce surrogates through all sorts of psychic experiences to which they ascribe the dignity of mystic holiness, which they peddle in the book market" (p. 154). Such activities, he wrote, are "plain humbug or self-deception" (pp. 154–155). Against the background of this kind of critical attitude, Moore, in his *The Re-Enchantment of Everyday Life* (1996), notes the difficulty of discussing enchantment in a disenchanted society (p. x) and the need continually to "defend the absurdity" and "suspect" nature of what he is writing (p. xi). Indeed, it is not clear that many of the strategies for reenchantment in his book—with their appeals to "communal fantasy life" (p. x), a "soft life of enchantment," whose "particulars" are "simple in comparison to the complexities of modern life" (p. xi)—are, for all their eloquence and charm, anything more than proposals for reattuning to states of naïve enchantment.

The kind of reenchantment that would correlate better with Jung's late-stage individuation is something fundamentally distinct from enchantment—or "naïve enchantment," as I have also been calling it. Such reenchantment is, as it were, on the other side of disenchantment, post- rather than pre-. Like late-stage individuation, the process of reenchantment is, in this understanding, a tremendously arduous and challenging task, to which everything Jung wrote about the difficulties and dangers of individuation might apply. "The attainment of wholeness [the goal of late-stage individuation and thus also the task of reenchantment] requires one to stake one's whole being," Jung stated. "Nothing less will do; there can be no easier conditions, no substitutes, no compromises" (1939/1969d, para. 906). This arduous process contrasts with any flight from disenchantment back into the more familiar, easier, and more comforting state of naïve enchantment. Such a flight would abandon the critical consciousness of disenchantment, whereas reenchantment, in the Jungian perspective, transcends such critical consciousness but in a way that still includes it. As Jung put it, "the instinct for wholeness"—that is, individuation—does not reject but precisely requires "a more highly differentiated consciousness, thoughtfulness, reflection, responsibility, and sundry other virtues" (1958/1970b, para. 653).

Such a process of reenchantment beyond disenchantment could perhaps be considered as the disenchanting of disenchantment, a process

30

of seeing through disenchantment as itself a fascination and fixation. In the expression used several times already, it entails breaking the spell of disenchantment. To be disenchanted even of disenchantment would be to allow other processes than empirical, rational, critical ones to arise or to become conscious precisely out of the limits and aporias of fully exercised empiricism and reason. Jung might have been intimating such a condition when, in the section of his *Red Book* (2009/2012) titled "The Magician," he describes how his visionary self, his "I," was baffled by the old magician Philemon's stymying of every attempt to understand magic rationally (pp. 395–406). Much later, in *Mysterium Coniunctionis* (1955–1956/1970a), Jung wrote more discursively about the paradoxical symbolism of alchemy (paras. 36–103), drew on the mystical languages of, among others, medieval Christianity, Taoism, Hinduism, and Buddhism (para. 771), and invoked the "magically effective action" and "magical qualities" of synchronicity (para. 758 and note 227). He hinted at a more participatory being in the world (para. 679, 753–755) and ultimately even at the possibility of mystical union with the ground of empirical reality (para. 771). The latter, as we have seen, can be conceived as a state of spontaneous creativity from which new enchanted realities might emerge. There seems little reason to suppose that these kinds of participatory and unitive states, which in the mystical literature usually require a lengthy, difficult, and even dangerous process of training and independent venture, should be effortlessly accessible when framed as aspects of reenchantment.

In sum, then, viewing individuation as a recursive process of enchantment–disenchantment–reenchantment can be helpful for understanding not just the overarching process of reenchantment but also the perpetual need for disenchantment and the continual presence of enchantment within that overarching process. Crucially, reenchantment, including its consummation in a state of mystical union, is needed to ground the entire process. Disenchantment will be incomplete until the spell it itself casts is also broken, and enchantments are likely to be inauthentic and ineffective if they are refuges from disenchantment rather than moments of spontaneous creativity arising in an openness beyond disenchantment.

JUNG, WEBER, AND THE *UNIO MYSTICA*

With the teasing out of these implications of individuation as a form of reenchantment that enfolds the related processes of enchantment and disenchantment, it might seem that we have strayed a long way from the academic world on which Weber was reflecting in "Science as a Vocation." In particular, the suggestion that individuation—and hence also the recursive process of enchantment–disenchantment–reenchantment— culminates and finds its grounding in a state of mystical union (*unio mystica*) will be academically beyond the pale for many. But before therefore locating Jung's psychology in an entirely different world of discourse from Weber's sociology, it is worth considering a recent reappraisal of Weber's position in relation to magic, religion, and especially mysticism.

In preparation, it is important to emphasize a few points about the state of mystical union as implicitly understood by Jung. First, while Jung's statements imply that the *unio mystica* is an ultimate and culminating state, it is not necessarily a final, once-and-for-all end-state. Those who claim to have experienced the *unio mystica*, perhaps including Jung (1963/1995, pp. 320–329; Main, 2021b), find that the state does not last forever—it may be an experience of eternity, but it is not an eternal experience. Again, the *unus mundus*, or "one world," with which the integrated spirit-mind-body is said to be conjoined is a "world of potential," and hence the *unio mystica* is not a final state of rest and stasis but a source of dynamic creativity and generativity; it continually brings the new and different into being (Main, 2021a, pp. 35–38).

Second, following from the first point, the state of unity or wholeness represented by the *unio mystica* does not provide a fixed point on which to establish hierarchical and totalitarian systems of ideas or values—a criticism sometimes leveled against claimed states of wholeness. Quite the contrary, the creative and generative dynamism of the state of *unio mystica* continually destabilizes all tendencies toward fixity and hierarchical structure. Its realization is not a refuge from challenge and change but rather an immersion in something difficult, dangerous, and requiring continual vigilance and readiness to change; in one sense, it is an immersion in the process of change itself (pp. 42–43).

Third, the state of *unio mystica* need not be understood only as a rare state involving the entirety of the personality. Insofar as the parts within a whole can themselves constitute wholes on another scale of consideration, as in Arthur Koestler's concept of the "holon" (1972, pp. 105–120), it is possible that Dorn's conjunctions, including the *unio mystica*, can be realized in relation to parts of the personality or partial experiences within it. For example, work on a particular dream image could result in the meaning of the image being realized in various ways: intrapsychically, integrating with one's present sense of psychic wholeness (*unio mentalis*); psychophysically, finding some realization, perhaps synchronistically, in one's embodied life (*caelum*); and cosmically, providing a momentary and partial expression of unitary reality (*unio mystica*).

Keeping in mind these qualifications about what mystical union might have meant for Jung, let us now return to Weber. The dominant image of Weber that emerges from "Science as a Vocation," as from Weber's work generally, is of someone who had regard for the tremendous historical significance of religion in shaping past and present social and economic formations across the world (1904–1905/2001, 1917–1919/1952a, 1915/1952b, 1916/1958) but who considered religious belief to be no longer viable in the modern West. To possess religion, he seems to be saying in "Science as a Vocation" (1919/1948d), it is necessary to forgo science and rationality by making an "intellectual sacrifice" (p. 155), and attempts to reconcile science and religion stem from a lack of either clarity or integrity. Weber himself recommended accepting the condition of disenchantment stoically, "like a man" (p. 155). Moreover, he famously described himself in a letter to Ferdinand Tönnies (19 February 1909) as "unmusical religiously" (cited in Josephson-Storm, 2017, p. 287).

It comes as a surprise, therefore, to learn that Weber may actually have taken great interest in, and attached great importance to, enchanted and in particular mystical states. The case for reconsidering Weber's relationship to mysticism stems mainly from the work of Jason Josephson-Storm (2017), drawing on the biography of Weber by Joachim Radkau (2009), who had access to letters and other personal documents not previously considered by scholars.

Josephson-Storm notes, in the first place, that Weber was far from unfamiliar with mysticism. Weber had remarked on the importance of Western mysticism already in *The Protestant Ethic and the Spirit of Capitalism* (1904–1905/2001, pp. 67, 193n66), and from around 1910, he began researching in depth into Chinese and Indian religions, taking particular interest in the fact that, in contrast to Protestantism, they had developed more mystical than ascetic outlooks (Josephson-Storm, 2017, pp. 275, 280). Around the same time, Weber also became acquainted with several contemporary mystics: above all, the poet Stefan George (1868–1933), the vitalist philosopher Ludwig Klages (1872–1956), and even members of the occult group Ordo Templi Orientis, whom he met during two month-long stays in spring 1913 and spring 1914 at the countercultural colony on Monte Verità, near Ascona in southern Switzerland (pp. 275, 290–293).

Moreover, argue both Radkau (2009, pp. 536–537) and Josephson-Storm (2017, pp. 287–289), Weber himself likely had mystical experiences and privately questioned whether he might not be a mystic. A key piece of evidence here is an exchange that Weber's nephew Eduard Baumgarten recorded between Weber and his wife, Marianne: "Tell me, can you imagine being a mystic?" Weber reportedly asked Marianne. "That's certainly the last thing I could imagine of myself," she replied, asking back: "Can you imagine it of yourself, then?" To which Weber responded: "It could be that I already am one . . ." (Radkau, 2009, p. 536; cf. Josephson-Storm, 2017, p. 289). Weber's scathing remarks about sham mysticism, suggested his friend Paul Honigsheim, probably stemmed from the fact that he knew "the genuine article" (Radkau, 2009, pp. 536–537; cf. Josephson-Storm, p. 289).

When Weber wrote about what he considered authentic mysticism, he generally did so in very positive terms. In *The Protestant Ethic* (1904–1905/2001), he referred to mysticism, specifically the *unio mystica*, as the "highest" form of religious experience (pp. 67, 193n66). Moreover, as Josephson-Storm remarks, when Weber later revised that work "with his concept of disenchantment in hand" (i.e., after 1913), he shifted from viewing mysticism as "a mere 'residual category'" to being "a living possibility comparable to asceticism" (2017, pp. 265–296). He may even have thought of mysticism, suggests Josephson-Storm, as "the last route to access the transcendent God expelled by reason" (p. 298). Far from being a sign of unmanliness, genuine mysticism even appears to have been for Weber a condition for wholesome being. In the same letter in which Weber, likely before any personal mystical experience, famously referred to his religious "unmusicality," he also made the following less often cited statement: "I see myself as a cripple, as a mutilated man whose inner destiny is to have to confess this [unmusicality] honestly" (p. 288). In other words, he considered that his never, up to that point (19 February 1909), having had a mystical experience made him "spiritually crippled" (p. 288).

Based on this evidence, Josephson-Storm argues that mysticism began to emerge in Weber's later works as a "paradoxical counterweight to rationalization" (p. 295):

> if one grants that some forms of mysticism are positive for Weber, one can see him working towards a set of oppositions: on one side, the alienation produced by bureaucracy, routinization, intellectual hyper-specialization; and on the other side, the potentially (but not necessarily) redemptive charisma, mysticism, and authentic prophecy. (p. 297)

Thus, in tension with the claimed incompatibility of science with religion that seems to emerge from "Science as a Vocation," Weber could also write, when revising *The Protestant Ethic*, that "religious belief which is primarily mystical may very well be compatible with a pronounced sense of reality in the field of empirical fact" (p. 67). Indeed, Josephson-Storm (2017) concludes that "what Weber was looking for was a higher-order synthesis, a return of enchantment or value in a higher key. This would be nothing less that the birth of a new religion" (p. 298). In sum, Weber "saw mysticism as a potential way out of disenchantment" (p. 289).

Weber died in 1920 at the age of 56. Whether he would have further and more publicly developed the above aspects of his thought had he lived longer is obviously unknown. As they stand, however, these hints of a potential way out of disenchantment point in precisely the directions pursued much more forthrightly—though not without his own ambivalence—by Jung. As we have seen, Jung offered through the process of individuation precisely a way out of disenchantment—a way, moreover, that, as in the hints from Weber, synthesizes disenchantment with enchantment, thereby involves the return of enchantment in a higher key, and is grounded in experience of the *unio mystica*. Notably, Jung's views received their first preliminary, visionary formulation in his *Red Book* (2009/2012), itself framed as a form of "authentic prophecy" (pp. 117–119) and mainly composed exactly at the time, between 1913 and 1917, when Weber was introducing the notions of enchantment and disenchantment into his own work.

CONCLUSION

In the 100 and more years since Weber wrote "Science as a Vocation" the narrative of disenchantment has exercised a powerful grip on Western culture—especially scientific, academic, and intellectual culture—and responses to the narrative, as we have seen, have been diverse. Jung's response was one of recognizing the overarching condition of disenchantment, with its ambivalent consequences and implications, and articulating a process of psychological transformation—individuation—aimed at overcoming that condition.

However, while thoroughly and sometimes urgently "breaking the spell of disenchantment" through affirming genuine mystery, inherent meaning, and metaphysical or spiritual reality, individuation for Jung nevertheless also continued to enfold what was valuable about disenchantment. Indeed, I have argued that recognizing a continuing interplay of enchantment, disenchantment, and reenchantment within the process of individuation can be helpful for understanding the complexity and ambivalence of other responses to disenchantment.

Jung's process of individuation, like many other attempts at reenchantment, is profoundly holistic, aiming as it does at realization of the self, the archetype of wholeness, and the culminating stage of this realization for Jung was experience of the *unio mystica*. Surprisingly, recent scholarship has suggested that Weber also envisaged the possibility of escaping disenchantment through experience of the *unio mystica*. However, Weber does not appear to have believed that authentic mystical experience, and the corresponding authentic prophecies and revelations that can be accessed through such experiences, are possible in the current prophetless age.

It remains questionable whether Weber would have considered the "prophecy" offered by Jung authentic, either as embodied by the charismatic figure of Jung himself or as subsequently routinized in the practice of analytical psychology. But the unexpected convergence of Weber and Jung in the concept of the *unio mystica* at least raises the possibility of developing forms of enchanted or reenchanted psychosocial studies, that is to say, forms of exploring and reflecting on psychological and social phenomena and their interactions that remain open to the possibilities of genuine mystery, inherent meaning, and relationship to transpersonal realities.

Be that as it may, Jung is unequivocal that the disenchanted perspective on reality, despite its many beneficial consequences, is limited and, if left to dominate, ultimately pernicious. The remaining chapters of this book examine some of the ways in which Jung, contrary to the disenchanted perspective, attempted to affirm genuine mystery, inherent meaning, and relationship to spiritual, divine, or metaphysical realities. We start with his affirmation of mystery.

ENDNOTES

[1] Nevertheless, as Jung's *Black Books* reveal, he was still actively engaged in his encounters with the unconscious at this time, dialoguing with the figures of Philemon, Ha, and Ka (Jung, 2020, pp. 147–170 [v. 7]). He had also recently begun to formulate his concept of the self, which had emerged from his drawing of numerous mandalas during his military service in Château d'Oex in autumn 1917 (Shamdasani, 2020, p. 61 [v. 1]; Jung, 2020, pp. 122–129 [v1]; p. 291n332 [v. 6]).

[2] The above account of the epistemological implications of disenchantment is based on the analysis by Egil Asprem in his book *The Problem of Disenchantment: Naturalism and Esoteric Discourse, 1900–1939* (2014, pp. 32–40). Asprem dubs the view that the world has been stripped of mystery "epistemological optimism"; the view that there is no inherent meaning in the world "axiological scepticism"; the view that the world is unrelated to any spiritual or divine realities "metaphysical scepticism"; and the view that science and religion are irreconcilable "the need for 'intellectual sacrifice' to possess religion" (p. 36). A complementary analysis can be found in Jason Josephson-Storm, *The Myth of Disenchantment: Magic, Modernity, and the Birth of the Human Sciences* (2017, p. 286). Both these books have been important sources for the present work.

[3] The first Jungian use of the term "disenchanted" that I have found appears in Marie-Louise von Franz's (1964, p. 228) essay, written in English, on "The Process of Individuation" in *Man and His Symbols* (Jung, 1964), the book Jung conceived, edited, and contributed to in the last two years of his life.

[4] Berman's (1981) book title appears to have been the first major use of the term "reenchantment."

Endnotes

5 The contributors to Landy and Saler's (2009) book find this phenomenon in fields as diverse as science, philosophy, linguistics, architecture, poetry, serial fiction, sport, and politics, as well as in individual responses to homelessness and other negative life events (pp. 7–14).

6 The third conjunction is discussed in detail elsewhere in Stein's work (e.g., 2014, pp. 122–126; 2019).

7 The difference between the psychotherapeutic and alchemical models may also suggest that the recursive process of enchantment–disenchantment–reenchantment can be understood "fractally," that is, as operating in a self-similar way at different scales. This is implicit in thinking about enchantment, disenchantment, and reenchantment as processes that could occur either at the sociocultural level or at the individual level. Similarly, the whole recursive process of enchantment, disenchantment, and reenchantment might operate either over the whole course of a life, as in the psychotherapeutic model, or within a particular stage of life, as in the alchemical model. Indeed, it arguably could operate at the scale of individual events within any stage. For example, there could be enchanted, disenchanted, and reenchanted phases within a relationship—developing from "emotional ties," to "withdraw[ing] these projections," to "the real *coniunctio*" (Jung, 1963/1995, p. 328); or within the interpretation of a dream—developing from identification with dream imagery, to the cognitive grasp of its meaning, to the realization of its meaning in life.

8 More in-depth discussions of Jung's challenges to the dimensions of disenchantment, focusing on selected aspects of his psychological project, will occur in chapters 2, 3, and 4.

9 The preceding stages bear comparison with what Robert Segal (1992) calls Jung's "History of the Psyche" (pp. 11–18): the state of mind of "primitives" in Segal's account parallels the state of enchantment, dominated by *participation mystique*"; that of "ancients" parallels the transition from enchantment to disenchantment, where there is a shift from identification to projection; that of "moderns" parallels the state of disenchantment, in which projections are increasingly withdrawn; and that of "contemporaries" parallels the state of reenchantment, in which

there is a conscious reconnection with the unconscious. Segal's formulation does not consider the possible unitive state of the *unio mystica* or the process of recursion.

10 For scholarly discussions of one of the culturally most widely disseminated expressions of such currents of reenchantment, so-called "New Age religions," see Heelas (1996), Hanegraaff (1998), and Sutcliffe and Gilhus (2014).

2

Mystery

When Max Weber (1919/1948d) claimed that the modern world is characterized by "intellectualist rationalization, created by science and by scientifically oriented technology" (p. 139), he was referring above all to a change of attitude toward how, compared with our ancestors, we acquire and deploy knowledge. As he put it:

> it means that principally there are no mysterious incalculable forces that come into play but rather that one can, in principle, master all things by calculation. This means that the world is disenchanted. One need no longer have recourse to magical means in order to master or implore the spirits, as did the savage for whom such mysterious powers existed. Technical means and calculations perform the service. (p. 139)[1]

In his summary of the philosophical implications of Weber's notion of disenchantment, Egil Asprem (2014) describes this position as "epistemological optimism," the belief that "Nature can in principle be understood by empiricism and reason" (p. 36). Jason Josephson-Storm (2017) similarly refers to this feature of disenchantment as a state of "epistemic overconfidence," that is, "the belief that everything can be known by means of intellectualization/theoretical rationality" (p. 286).

In this chapter, we shall look at Jung's lifelong preoccupation with phenomena that seem particularly suggestive of "mysterious incalculable forces" and thus resistant to explanation in terms of calculation, empiricism, and theoretical rationality. The phenomena in question have been variously called mysterious, occult, spiritualistic, paranormal, parapsychological, exceptional, wild, rogue, or, as I prefer, anomalous. I shall first indicate the extent and range of Jung's studies and experiences of these phenomena, whose general nature will become apparent from brief accounts of some of Jung's experiences of them. I shall then discuss the concept of synchronicity, which Jung developed to explain such phenomena, looking especially at how this concept focuses attention on their meaning. Finally, I shall highlight Jung's social motivation for engaging with anomalous phenomena, which I primarily locate in his attempt to foster a reenchantment, or, as he termed it, a resacralization, of the world and thereby help to address the spiritual crisis of modernity.

Jung's interest in anomalous phenomena was by no means idiosyncratic. Such phenomena attracted the attention of many others influential in the early development of psychology and depth psychology, including Pierre Janet (1859–1947), Frederic Myers (1843–1901), William James (1842–1910), Granville Stanley Hall (1846–1924), Theodore Flournoy (1854–1920), Eugen Bleuler (1857–1939), Sigmund Freud, and Sandor Ferenczi (1873–1933) (Main, 2015, pp. 736–738). Nor have such interests been of solely historical interest. Since the founding of the Society for Psychical Research in 1882 and the development of the discipline of experimental parapsychology by Joseph Banks Rhine (1895–1980) and others around 1930, paranormal phenomena have been an object of regular, if usually underfunded, scientific scrutiny in many countries. For example, particularly important work has been done in these areas over the last two decades by Edward Kelly and colleagues and reported and reflected on in a series of three compendious volumes (Kelly et al., 2007, 2015, 2021). This work, based on rigorous research in the sciences and high-quality scholarship in the humanities, has focused on data that present challenges to the dominant worldview of materialism or physicalism, with the connections between that worldview and the experience of disenchantment clearly stated (2015, p. 542; 2021, pp. 2, 484, 486).

There are several distinctive features of Jung's approach to anomalous phenomena that are important to highlight at the outset. First, most psychical researchers and parapsychologists have been preoccupied with the questions of how to demonstrate the reality of anomalous phenomena and how to explain the mechanisms of their occurrence.[2] Jung, by contrast, approached these phenomena in a way that, while not disregarding issues of proof and explanation, focused instead on the question of what anomalous phenomena *mean*—for the individuals who experience them and, more widely, for society and culture. The issue of meaning, raised in the present chapter in relation to anomalous phenomena, will be taken up and explored more deeply in Chapter 3.

Second, Jung provided an instance of at least the *kind* of model within which anomalous phenomena and their meaning might be comprehended—a psychological, and ultimately psychophysical, model aimed at providing a view of the total human personality and, as such, thoroughly holistic (McMillan et al., 2020; Main et al., 2021). Jung's is, moreover, a model in which the propensity to experience and believe in anomalous phenomena need not be considered pathological. Ultimately, Jung's holistic model is grounded in a metaphysical view that, like the approaches explored by Kelly and colleagues (2015), challenges the physicalism and/or implicit substance dualism underpinning mainstream science—an issue that will be explored in Chapter 4.

Third, Jung maintained an open-minded position on the relationship between science and the nonrational. He endeavored to keep his psychological model as much as possible in continuity with mainstream science, and he never tired of characterizing himself as a scientist (e.g., 1973a, p. 227; 1976, p. 567). But his primary commitment was to the phenomena he encountered, and insofar as these included anomalous phenomena, his psychological model and view of reality were developed to accommodate them and were deeply shaped by them (Main, 1997, pp. 1–44). As a result, his model ended up challenging some of the assumptions of mainstream scientific psychology and proposing how science in general might need to be expanded (Main, 2004, pp. 121–129)— a step that many other researchers, including Kelly and colleagues (2007, 2015, 2021), have concluded will need to be taken, in one way or another, by any adequate theory of anomalous phenomena.

A fourth and final feature that is distinctive about Jung's model is that it helps to locate anomalous phenomena in broader social and cultural as well as personal contexts. As the scholar of religions Jeffrey Kripal has noted, paranormal or anomalous experiences have had and continue to have enormous social and cultural influence. On the one hand, they are at the root of many of the religions and myths, mainstream as well as heterodox, that have been most influential in world history (Kripal et al., 2014). On the other hand, they are ubiquitous in present-day popular culture (Kripal, 2011; cf. Partridge, 2004, 2014). Jung's thought acknowledges these past and present contexts and also provides a theoretical framework for deeply understanding them. In part, Jung's psychological model can account for the social and cultural significance of anomalous phenomena because, with its concept of the collective unconscious, it is inherently collective as well as individual, so that what appears to be simply a personal anomalous experience may express a pattern of meaning that is of much wider social and cultural significance (1963/1995, pp. 199–201). Especially pertinent for the present discussion is that Jung's interest in anomalous phenomena seems to have been deeply influenced by his concern for the disenchanted condition of modern society and culture (Main, 2004, p. 138; 2013a; 2013c; 2017), and it is on this in particular that I focus in the present chapter.

JUNG'S STUDIES AND EXPERIENCES OF ANOMALOUS PHENOMENA

As a student, Jung read extensively in the literature of psychical research (1963/1995, p. 120), and one of the student lectures he delivered to his fraternity, the Zofingia Society, was an impassioned appeal for the serious scientific study of spiritualistic phenomena (Jung, 1896–1899/1983, paras. 67–142; Oeri, 1970, pp. 187–188). His own first effort at such study resulted in his doctoral dissertation, "On the Psychology and Pathology of So-Called Occult Phenomena" (1902/1957), which was based on close observations of his mediumistic cousin, Hélène Preiswerk (Charet, 1993, pp. 149–168). This interest continued during Jung's first professional appointment, as an intern at the Burghölzli Mental Hospital in Zurich, where he reported on his observations of several other mediums (1905/1977m), and there are also records of his attending séances in the 1920s and 1930s (Charet, 1993, pp. 282–283nn230–231). Aside from such observations, Jung conducted around 1920 an informal experiment with the Chinese divinatory system of the *I Ching*, later lamenting that he had not kept notes (1963/1995, pp. 407–408). He avidly followed the more quantitative, laboratory-based parapsychological work carried out by Rhine and his colleagues at Duke University from the 1930s, and he maintained an intermittent correspondence with Rhine between 1934 and 1954 (1973a, pp. 180–182, 378–379; Mansfield et al., 1998). Seemingly inspired by Rhine, Jung devised his own parapsychological experiment in which he collected large quantities of astrological data and subjected them to statistical analyses (1952/1969r, paras. 872–915). He also took a keen interest in the phenomenon of UFOs (Unidentified Flying Objects), on which he gathered reports and writings from the time of the phenomenon's public emergence around 1947 until his death in 1961 (1958/1970b). These and similar investigations, spanning the whole of Jung's professional life, led to his writing three book-length studies and over a dozen shorter papers relevant to psychical research and parapsychology.[3]

But Jung's engagement with this area was not restricted to study and writing. Fueling his interest were personal experiences of an extraordinary number and range of anomalous phenomena. These experiences, occurring throughout his long life, encompassed apparitions and poltergeists, spiritualistic communications and materializations, telepathic, clairvoyant, and precognitive dreams, prophetic and mystical visions, psychokinetic events, out-of-body and near-death experiences, and meaningful coincidences (Jung, 1963/1995; Main, 1997, 2012, 2021).

The range and nature of Jung's anomalous experiences can be illustrated by the following selection drawn from his posthumously published *Memories, Dreams, Reflections* (1963/1995).[4] The incidents date from the first half of Jung's life (up to the age of 41) before he had clearly set down his mature psychological theory or worked out the concept of synchronicity that he would later invoke to make sense of such experiences. Indeed, the experiences were arguably formative on the nature of the theory and concepts he would develop, which needed to be adequate to explain such experiences. The experiences also all antedate Weber's lecture "Science as a Vocation," in which the German sociologist most famously deployed the notion of disenchantment.

Apparition with Detaching Heads

The earliest of Jung's anomalous experiences of which we have a record occurred when he was 7 or 8. During a period when his parents were sleeping apart and there was considerable tension in the house, he reports that he would sometimes see nocturnal apparitions:

> One night I saw coming from [my mother's] door a faintly luminous, indefinite figure whose head detached itself from the neck and floated along in front of it, in the air, like a little moon. Immediately another head was produced and again detached itself. This process was repeated six or seven times. (1963/1995, pp. 33–34)

Splitting Table and Exploding Knife

More spectacularly, when Jung was 23 and by that time a medical student, a round walnut table in his family home suddenly and inexplicably split against the grain with a loud bang, in the hearing of his mother, their maid, and himself (1963/1995, pp. 125–126; 1973a, p. 181). Around the same time, another loud explosion was heard in Jung's home, and it was discovered that a steel knife that was in perfect condition and had been used to cut bread just an hour earlier had shattered into four in a closed drawer. In the breadbasket Jung found "a loaf of bread, and, beside it, the bread knife. The greater part of the blade," he reports, "had snapped off in several pieces. The handle lay in one corner of the rectangular basket and in each of the other corners lay a piece of the blade" (1963/1995, pp. 126–127; 1973a, p. 181).

Detonating Bookcase

Possibly the most famous of Jung's anomalous experiences occurred in Freud's study when Jung visited Freud in 1909. In the course of an argument about anomalous phenomena, Jung relates that he felt as if his diaphragm were "made of iron and were becoming red-hot—a glowing vault." He continues:

> [A]t that moment there was such a loud report in the bookcase, which stood right next to us, that we both started up in alarm, fearing that the thing was going to topple over on us. I said to Freud: "There, that is an example of a so-called catalytic exteriorization phenomenon."
>
> "Oh come," he exclaimed. "That is sheer bosh."
>
> "It is not," I replied. "You are mistaken, Herr Professor. And to prove my point I now predict that in a moment there will be another loud report!" Sure enough, no sooner had I said the words than the same detonation went off in the bookcase. (1963/1995, pp. 178–179; McGuire, 1974, pp. 218–220)

Prophetic Visions

Following his break with Freud in 1913, Jung experienced, between October 1913 and July 1914, a series of disturbing visions. In these, he saw monstrous floods across Europe, civilization reduced to rubble, thousands of drowned bodies, and the sea turning to blood (1963/1995, pp. 199–201; 1990, pp. 41–44; 2009/2012, pp. 123–125). He had a three-times-repeated dream of the land frozen in summer beneath an Arctic cold wave, though on the third occurrence, he saw himself plucking grapes "full of healing juices" and giving them to "a large waiting crowd." At first, Jung suspected that these images referred to him and indicated an emerging psychosis. However, when the First World War broke out in August 1914, he immediately came to view them as prophetic and of more collective and social significance (1963/1995, pp. 200–201; 2009/2012, p. 123).

Kingfisher Coincidence

Jung soon developed techniques for engaging with his visionary experiences and positively encouraging them for what they could reveal about the unconscious mind. Prominent among the experiences cultivated in this way were his inner encounters with a variety of seemingly autonomous fantasy figures with whom he conversed as though they were spirits (1963/1995, pp. 201–210). The most important such figure was "Philemon," whom Jung described as his "ghostly guru," his "psychagogue," a representation of "superior insight" who, he says, "conveyed to me many an illuminating idea" (pp. 207–208; 2009/2012, pp. 395–412). On one occasion Philemon appeared in Jung's dreams with kingfisher's wings, and Jung, in order to understand the image better, did a painting of it. While engaged in this, he happened to find in his garden, for the first and only time, a dead kingfisher (1963/1995, pp. 207–208).

Haunting of Jung's House

Later, in 1916, Jung relates that he felt "compelled from within, as it were, to formulate and express what might have been said by Philemon" (1963/1995, p. 215). The composition of the resulting *Septem Sermones ad Mortuos*, a series of texts addressed to the spirits of the dead, was immediately preceded by a remarkable haunting of Jung's house:

> My eldest daughter saw a white figure passing through the room. My second daughter, independently of her elder sister, related that twice in the night her blanket had been snatched away; and that same night my nine-year-old son had an anxiety dream. In the morning he asked his mother for crayons, and he, who ordinarily never drew, now made a picture of his dream. He called it "The Picture of the Fisherman." [...][5]
>
> Around five o'clock in the afternoon on Sunday the front-door bell began ringing frantically. It was a bright summer day; the two maids were in the kitchen, from which the open square outside the front door could be seen. Everyone immediately

looked to see who was there, but there was no one in sight. I was sitting near the door bell, and not only heard it but saw it moving. We all simply stared at one another. (pp. 215–216)

Jung had the sense that the house was "crammed full of spirits," but as soon as he began to write the text that became *Septem Sermones* "the whole ghostly assemblage vanished" (p. 216).

Corroborating Details

Jung did not present himself as naively enchanted by these experiences but as perplexed and critical. In *Memories, Dreams, Reflections* (1963/1995), he both highlights their anomalousness and reports his attempts, mostly failed, to explain the experiences in terms of common sense or established science. For example, his narratives include detail clearly intended to corroborate that what he says took place did and was indeed anomalous. "A table of solid walnut that had dried out for seventy years—how," he asks, "could it split on a summer day in the relatively high humidity characteristic of our climate?" (p. 126) He relates that he took the pieces of the bread knife to a cutler to determine under what conditions it could have broken as it did and was assured that it could not have done so spontaneously (p. 127). When recounting this episode later to Rhine, he added:

> No traces of tearing or cutting were found on the sides of the basket nor in the loaf of bread, so that the explosive force apparently did not exceed that amount of energy which was just needed to break the knife and was completely exhausted with the breaking itself. (1973a, p. 181)

Jung kept the fragments of the knife and sent a photograph of them to Rhine (pp. 180–182). Again, to highlight the anomalousness of the kingfisher coincidence, Jung notes that kingfishers are rare in the vicinity of Zurich, that he had never since found a dead one, and that the one he did find was recently dead (1963/1995, p. 207). In relation to other experiences, he stresses the number of witnesses involved: the splitting table was witnessed by his mother, their maid, and himself (pp. 125–126); the exploding knife by his mother, his 14-year-old sister, and their maid (p. 126); and the mysteriously ringing doorbell by his entire household, including at least two of his daughters, his son, two maids, and himself (p. 215).

The details of this kind that Jung provides fall far short of the kind of proof that would convince a skeptic. But they do serve to show Jung's awareness of the issue of proof and thereby add rhetorically to the prima facie plausibility of his narratives.[6] They evince both his sensitivity to the disenchanted culture that would receive the accounts and his own critical consciousness that wished to explain the experiences in terms of empiricism and reason. That he could not plausibly explain them is what, for him, established them as mysterious.

SYNCHRONICITY AS A FRAMEWORK FOR UNDERSTANDING ANOMALOUS PHENOMENA

The experiences described above all occurred before Jung had formulated his concept of synchronicity. And even though *Memories, Dreams, Reflections*, where the accounts are found, was compiled at the end of Jung's life, that text still contains no systematic attempt to explain the experiences in relation to synchronicity. This reticence may be due to the fact that Jung relates the experiences in a memoir, which he may have felt was not the place to enter into the necessary theoretical complexities. Be that as it may, since it was ultimately in relation to synchronicity that Jung later argued such events could be best understood, I shall now draw on his mature formulation of synchronicity to see what understanding or helpful perspectives it might be able to provide.[7]

Jung defined synchronicity in a variety of ways. Most succinctly, he defined it as "meaningful coincidence," as "an acausal connecting principle," or as "acausal parallelism" (1952/1969r, para. 827 and subtitle; 1963/1995, p. 407). More fully, he defined it as "the simultaneous occurrence of a certain psychic state with one or more external events which appear as meaningful parallels to the momentary subjective state" (1951/1969h, para. 850). An example of Jung's conveys what he means by these definitions as well as how the concept of synchronicity fits into his overall psychological model.

The example concerns a young woman patient whose excessive intellectuality, Jung says, made her "psychologically inaccessible," closed off from a "more human understanding" (1951/1969h, para. 982). Unable to make headway in analyzing her, Jung reports that he had to confine himself to "the hope that something unexpected would turn up, something that would burst the intellectual retort into which she had sealed herself" (para. 982). He continues:

> Well, I was sitting opposite her one day, with my back to the window, listening to her flow of rhetoric. She had had an impressive dream the night before, in which someone had given her a golden scarab—a costly piece of jewellery. While she was still telling me this dream, I heard something behind me gently tapping on the window. I turned round and saw that it was a fairly large flying insect that was knocking against the window-pane in the obvious effort to get into the dark room. This seemed to me very strange. I opened the window immediately and caught the insect in the air as it flew in. It was a scarabaeid beetle, or common rose-chafer (*Cetonia aurata*), whose gold-green colour most nearly resembles that of a golden scarab. I handed the beetle to my patient with the words, "Here is your scarab." This experience punctured the desired hole in her rationalism and broke the ice of her intellectual resistance. The treatment could now be continued with satisfactory results. (para. 982)

In this example, the *psychic state* is indicated by the patient's telling Jung her dream of being given a scarab. The *parallel external event* is the appearance and behavior of the real scarab. The telling of the dream and the appearance of the real scarab were *simultaneous*. Neither of these events discernibly or plausibly caused the other by any normal means, so their relationship is *acausal*. Nevertheless, the events parallel each other in such unlikely detail that one cannot escape the impression that they are indeed *connected*, albeit acausally. Moreover, this acausal connection of events both is symbolically informative (as we shall see) and has a deeply emotive and transformative effect on the patient and in these senses is clearly *meaningful*.

Jung attempted to account for synchronistic events primarily in terms of his concept of *archetypes*. For this purpose, he highlighted the nature of archetypes as "formal factors responsible for the organization of unconscious psychic processes: they are 'patterns of behaviour.' At the same time they have a 'specific charge' and develop numinous effects which express themselves as *affects*" (1952/1969r, para. 841). They "constitute the structure" not of the personal but "of the *collective unconscious* ... psyche that is identical in all individuals" (para. 840; emphasis added). Jung further characterized archetypes as psychoid on account of their being irrepresentable (para. 840) and able to manifest in outer physical processes as well as inner psychic ones (para. 964). Also relevant is that archetypes typically express themselves in the form of *symbolic images* (para. 845). Jung considered that synchronistic events tend to occur in situations in which an archetype is active or "constellated" (para. 847). Such constellation of archetypes in the life of a person is, as we saw in Chapter 1, governed by the process of *individuation*—in short, the inherent drive of the psyche toward increased wholeness and self-realization. Individuation in turn proceeds through the dynamic of *compensation*, whereby any one-sidedness in a person's conscious attitude is balanced by contents emerging from the unconscious which, if successfully integrated, contribute to a state of greater psychic wholeness.

Relating these psychological dynamics to his example, Jung suggested that it had "an archetypal foundation" (para. 845) and, more specifically, that it was the archetype of rebirth that was constellated. He wrote: "Any essential change of attitude signifies a psychic renewal which is usually accompanied by symbols of rebirth in the patient's dreams and fantasies. The scarab is a classic example of a rebirth symbol" (para. 845). The emotional charge or numinosity of the archetype is evident from its having "broke[n] the ice of [the patient's] intellectual resistance." The compensatory nature of the experience is also clear: The patient's one-sided rationalism and psychological stasis were counteracted by an event that both in its symbolism and in its action expressed the power of the irrational and the possibility of renewal. Finally, that all of this promoted the patient's individuation is implied by Jung's statement that "The treatment could now be continued with satisfactory results."

SYNCHRONICITY AND CATEGORIES OF ANOMALOUS PHENOMENA

While this example and analysis illustrate Jung's overall understanding of the kinds of events that compose synchronicities and what confers the meaning that elevates mere coincidences into synchronicities, Jung found it necessary to expand his definition still further. His most systematic attempt to pin down precisely what he understood by the term "synchronicity" was with the following three-pronged definition. An event fitting into one or other of these three categories is synchronistic:

1. The coincidence of a psychic state in the observer with a simultaneous, objective, external event that corresponds to the psychic state or content (e.g., the scarab), where there is no evidence of a causal connection between the psychic state and the external event, and where, considering the psychic relativity of space and time, such a connection is not even conceivable.
2. The coincidence of a psychic state with a corresponding (more or less simultaneous) external event taking place outside the observer's field of perception, i.e., at a distance, and only verifiable afterward ....
3. The coincidence of a psychic state with a corresponding, not yet existent future event that is distant in time and likewise can only be verified afterward. (1951/1969h, para. 984)[8]

The second and third prongs of the above definition aim to capture cases in which the coinciding external event occurs either at a distance or in the future (giving "clairvoyant" or "telepathic" and "precognitive" coincidences, respectively). An example of the former is Emmanuel Swedenborg's famous vision in which he "saw," in subsequently verified detail, the progress of a fire in Stockholm 200 miles away at the same time as it was happening (1952/1969r, para. 912). An instance of the precognitive kind of coincidence would be the case mentioned by Jung of a student friend of his whose father had promised him a trip to Spain if he passed his final examinations satisfactorily. The friend then had a dream of seeing various things in a Spanish city: a particular square, a Gothic cathedral, and, around a certain corner, a carriage drawn by two cream-colored horses. Later, having successfully passed his examinations, he visited Spain for the first time and encountered in physical reality all the details from his dream (1951/1969h, para. 973).

As he wrote to Rhine on 9 August 1954, Jung believed that "all forms of ESP [extra-sensory perception] (telepathy, precognition, etc.) including PK [psychokinesis] have essentially the same underlying principle, viz. the identity of a subjective and an objective arrangement coinciding in time (hence the term 'synchronicity')" (1976, p. 181). He considered the concepts of telepathy, clairvoyance, and precognition to be "purely descriptive": "These concepts naturally have no explanatory value as each of them represents an X which cannot be distinguished from the X of the other. The characteristic feature of all these phenomena, including Rhine's psychokinetic effect ..., is *meaningful coincidence*, and as such I have defined the synchronistic principle" (1955–1956/1970a, para. 662).

To account for psychokinesis, Jung highlighted the phrase "the psychic relativity of space and time" embedded in the first part of the three-pronged definition above: "[Rhine's] experiment with dice [i.e., his psychokinetic experiment] proves that moving bodies ... can be influenced psychically—a result that could have been predicted from the psychic relativity of space and time" (1951/1969h, para. 978). For, Jung argues, "If space and time prove to be psychically relative, then the moving body must possess, or be subject to, a corresponding relativity" (1952/1969r, para. 837). When asked by Wolfgang Pauli for clarification about this point, Jung elaborated that "The psychic 'relativity of mass' is actually a logical outcome of the psychic relativity of time and space, insofar as mass cannot be defined without a concept of space and, when it is moved, not without a concept of time" (Meier, 2001, p. 62). How this might help to account for psychokinesis remains difficult to grasp. But perhaps one way of under-standing Jung's thinking is that the relativization of space and time could allow the physical conditions required for the occurrence of the anomalous physical component of a psychokinetic event (the behavior of a particular mass) to be spontaneously, acausally, present at a time and in a place from which they had been absent.[9]

Jung summarized his position in his essay "On the Nature of the Psyche" (1947/1954/1969g), where he states, "The very diverse and confusing aspects of these [parapsychological] phenomena are, so far as I can see at present, completely explicable on the assumption of a psychically relative space-time continuum" (para. 440). His main reason for believing that space and time are psychically relative was, in fact, the results of Rhine's experiments. For Jung, these experiments showed that "in relation to the psyche space and time are, so to speak, elastic and can apparently be reduced almost to vanishing point, as though they were dependent on psychic conditions and did not exist in themselves but were only 'postulated' by the conscious mind" (1952/1969r, para. 840). To avoid the circularity of explaining Rhine's results with a principle derived from those results, Jung refers for corroboration both to primitive views of the world in which "space and time have a very precarious existence," becoming "'fixed' concepts" only with the introduction of measurement, and to Kantian philosophy, which regards the categories of space and time as "created by the intellectual needs of the observer" (para. 840). Both this fixing of concepts through measurement and this creation of categories for the intellectual needs of the observer again evoke the process of disenchantment with which Jung's concept of synchronicity was arguably engaging.

SYNCHRONICITY AND JUNG'S ANOMALOUS EXPERIENCES

For Jung, then, synchronicity can in principle account for all the main categories of anomalous phenomena. In practice, though, even the concept of synchronicity remains under pressure from the mysterious phenomenology of anomalous experiences. In relation to the selection of Jung's experiences described above, the concept of synchronicity most neatly fits those in which inner visions and images coincide with outer physical events that nonetheless seem to have naturalistic causes. These include the prophetic visions, where Jung's inner fantasies seemed to prefigure political events in Europe, and the kingfisher coincidence, which has a structure very similar to that of Jung's paradigmatic synchronicity involving the scarab.

However, the concept of synchronicity seems less immediately applicable to apparitions, where there are no related physical phenomena. Among Jung's experiences, this includes the apparition with detaching heads, the encounters with Philemon, and (through report) the ghost seen by Jung's daughter. It is quite possible that these inner "images" do match outer, physical events. For example, the apparition with detaching heads may well have symbolized an actual state of dissociation of Jung's mother or of separation in his parents' marital relationship. But if this is the case, it would be difficult to establish that the relationship was not rather a causal one, the apparition having been generated causally, if psychologically, by Jung's unconscious perceptions and mental states.

The account of the ghost seen by Jung's daughter is embedded within a wider narrative in which related physical phenomena (the invisible snatching of her sister's blanket and the mysteriously ringing doorbell) also figure, but these physical events, as we shall see, present their own difficulties, and it is primarily the apparitional and poltergeist events individually rather than any coincidental relationship between them that evoke the sense of the anomalous.

Jung's visionary encounters with Philemon are interesting in that, in describing them, Jung stresses the reality of the apparitional figure. "It was he [Philemon]," Jung writes, "who taught me psychic objectivity, the reality of the psyche" (1963/1995, p. 208), that is, "that there are things in the psyche which I do not produce, but which produce themselves and have their own life" (p. 207). This psychic objectivity included his, Philemon's, own objectivity: "At times he seemed to me quite real, as if he were a living personality. I went walking up and down the garden with him ..." (p. 208).

Regarding the objective existence of spirits, Jung recalled to a correspondent in 1946 his discussions many years earlier with the American psychologist and psychical researcher James Hyslop:

> He [Hyslop] admitted that, all things considered, all these metapsychic phenomena could be explained better by the hypothesis of spirits than by the qualities and peculiarities of the unconscious. And here, on the basis of my own experience, I am bound to concede he is right. In each individual case I must of necessity be sceptical, but in the long run I have to admit that the spirit hypothesis yields better results in practice than any other. (1973a, p. 431)

It is not clear from the definitions above—or from Jung's writings generally—how the concept of synchronicity would account for the objective existence of spirits. The objective existence of spirits seems rather to be a competing or complementary hypothesis, which could be invoked to explain some kinds of meaningful coincidences.

The concept of synchronicity also has some difficulty explaining phenomena where physical events occur with no apparent naturalistic cause. Among Jung's experiences, this includes the splitting table, exploding knife, detonating bookcase, snatched blanket, and ringing doorbell. Each of these outer events coincided meaningfully with an intense psychic state, and so the composite event does meet the criterion for being accounted synchronistic. But it is primarily the physical events themselves, with their apparent lack of naturalistic cause, that produce the anomalous effect and most immediately attract attention. The concept of synchronicity does not aim to account for the component events of a coincidence but only for the relationship between them. Jung, as we have seen, tries to relate such psychokinetic or poltergeist phenomena to synchronicity through his notion of the psychic relativity of space and time. But it has to be said that his brief comments on this read like afterthoughts and seem insufficient to carry the weight of what is implied by the extraordinary phenomena in question. Pauli, who as a leading physicist knew a thing or two about relativity, considered Jung's argument about the psychic relativity of space and time and, by implication, of moving bodies to be "very obscure," even after Jung had responded to his request for clarification (Meier, 2001, pp. 58, 62–63, 67). As we shall see in the next chapter, these perplexities did not prevent Pauli from agreeing with Jung about the potential of the concept of synchronicity for addressing disenchantment.[10]

JUNG'S FOCUS ON THE MEANING OF ANOMALOUS PHENOMENA

The concept of synchronicity attaches equal importance to the inner psychic and the outer physical components of a synchronistic event. Since many anomalous experiences occur that seem primarily inner and psychic or primarily outer and physical, the concept of synchronicity serves to draw attention to the complementary outer physical or inner psychic aspect, respectively. In this way, it arguably spurs a more holistic view of the phenomena. More particularly, it focuses attention on the meaning that, in the absence of a discernible or plausible causal relationship, is what connects the inner psychic and outer physical events. We shall discuss more fully in Chapter 3 how Jung understands meaning in relation to synchronicity, which is a complex and controversial topic deeply implicated with his thinking about archetypes. For present purposes, we can distinguish two main levels of meaning that are relevant to Jung's discussions: the personal level, which concerns the events and aims of Jung's life individually; and the collective level, which concerns events and patterns of meaning that seem to be of more than personal relevance.

THE MEANING OF JUNG'S ANOMALOUS EXPERIENCES

We can make only tentative and speculative suggestions about what the anomalous experiences described above might have meant either personally to Jung or more collectively, since they are included within Jung's memoir for particular narrative purposes and do not include the level of contextual information that would be required for a more confident analysis—quite apart from the fact that Jung is no longer around to respond to any proposed interpretations. Nevertheless, some observations can be made that may suffice at least to indicate the general value of focusing attention on the factor of meaning.

Personal Meaning

At a personal level, we can note that each of Jung's experiences occurred against a deep emotional background and at what turned out to be critical junctures in his life. The apparition with the detaching heads occurred during a period when there appear to have been especially acute difficulties in Jung's parents' marriage, which cannot but have affected the 7- or 8-year-old child. The episodes of the splitting walnut table and the exploding bread knife occurred at a time when, in difficult economic circumstances, Jung had to make a choice of career; in relation to this choice, he writes that the experiences were "destined to influence me profoundly" (1963/1995, p. 125; cf. p. 128). Specifically, they seem to have consolidated his interest in spiritualistic phenomena and may have contributed to his decision to intensify his observations of his mediumistic cousin and use them as the basis of his doctoral dissertation (p. 127).[11] In the context of his interest in spiritualism, it is probably relevant that Jung's father had died just 18 months earlier and that the walnut table had come from the dowry of Jung's paternal grandmother (pp. 116, 126). It is also worth noting the comment of Jung's mother about the splitting table— "that means something" (p, 126)—and Jung's annoyance at being unable to find anything to say in response.

No less crucial to Jung was the emotional background to his experience of the detonating bookcase, in which his relationship with Freud, probably the most significant professional relationship in Jung's life, showed one of the fissures along which it would eventually, ineluctably split. Moreover, this happened just at the time when Freud, by his own account, had "adopted" Jung as his "eldest son" and "anointed" him as his "successor and crown prince" (McGuire, 1974, p. 218). Similarly, Jung's prophetic visions occurred during his profound sense of disorientation following the split from Freud, when Jung feared he might be going mad.

It marked a moment of realization of the more than personal significance of his inner experiences. Finally, the haunting of Jung's house occurred at another turning point within his disorientation, when he articulated in the *Septem Sermones ad Mortuos*, albeit in "peculiar language" (1963/1995, p. 215), the outlines of the psychological model that he would develop over the coming years and decades (Charet, 1993, pp. 265–267).

Collective Meaning

When we look for the possible meaning of Jung's experiences at a more collective level, we are on even shakier ground. Many would not accept Jung's premises that such meaning is there to be found even in principle, and even if we are willing to entertain the possibility, it is not at all clear what would constitute sufficient evidence for or even a convincing indication of any particular interpretation. Moreover, analysts have long recognized the difficulty of distinguishing in practice between personal and collective levels of significance of psychic contents, even when they accept the distinction in principle (Williams, 1963). Nevertheless, we can again cautiously point to some themes that at least give an outline of what a collective level of interpretation might look like. As a way of attempting to transcend the subjective particularities and context dependence of the individual incidents, I shall focus on themes that seem to be exhibited by several, even if not all, of the incidents described.

One theme that immediately stands out from several of the experiences is that of *splitting and fragmentation*. The head of the apparition *detaches* itself in a context where Jung's parents are sleeping *apart*, the round walnut table *splits*, the bread knife *shatters into fragments* in the basket, and the detonating bookcase signals a *fissure* in Jung's relationship with Freud. Interestingly, much of the symbolism here plays a central role in Jung's mature writings. For example, detached heads, significant in relation to various oracles and rites of transformation, appear in Jung's religious and alchemical writings (1938/1954/1968j, para. 95; 1942/1954/1969t, paras. 365–373; 1955–1956/1970a, paras. 626, 730). Images of round objects, including round tables, are of paramount importance for him as mandalas—symbols of synthesis, union, and wholeness (1942/1954/1969t, para. 418; 1944/1968c, paras. 122–331, especially 242n118, 238, 241, 260). Quaternary images, of which we might see as an example Jung's rectangular breadbasket with a fragment of the shattered knife in each of its four corners, similarly appear as symbols of wholeness (1942/1948/1969i, paras. 243–285). In general, Jung's experiences present images of wholeness broken. His life's work was largely about discovering and fostering a psychological process—individuation—for bringing about or restoring wholeness.

Another symbolic theme discernible in Jung's experiences is that of *death and reanimation*, applied to both individuals and environments. Jung associates the splitting table and exploding knife with *his father's death* and with the spiritualistic séances, that is, *attempts to communicate with and in that sense "reanimate" the dead*, in which he participated and about which he subsequently wrote.

Following the incident of the detonating bookcase, Freud wrote to Jung offering his own naturalistic and skeptical account of the event in terms of creaking furniture and the "spell" of Jung's "personal presence" (McGuire, 1974, pp. 218–220; Jung, 1963/1995, pp. 397–399). Alluding to a famous expression in a poem by Friedrich Schiller (1759–1805), which was one of the sources of Weber's notion of disenchantment,[12] Freud asserts, "The furniture stands before me *spiritless and dead*, like nature silent and godless before the poet after *the passing of the gods* of Greece" (McGuire, 1974, p. 218, emphasis added; Jung, 1963/1995, p. 397).[13] This reveals his assumption that, by contrast, Jung considered the furniture *mysteriously animated and communicative*.

Again, Jung's prophetic visions present landscapes of *destruction, sterility, and death*, yet with the promise of *renewal* in the image of "sweet grapes full of healing juices" (1963/1995, p. 200). The kingfisher coincidence involves finding *a dead bird*, which paradoxically helps to affirm for Jung the *living reality* of his "*ghostly* guru [emphasis added]" Philemon. And the account of the haunting of Jung's house presents *the dead* as themselves *animatedly striving to communicate* with the living—ringing at the door, snatching a blanket away from one who would sleep and remain unconscious of them, and impelling both Jung and his son to give expression to inner images.

The Motif of the Grail Legend

Especially interesting in the haunting is the son's drawing, "The Picture of the Fisherman." Later in life, especially in his book *Aion* (1951/1968b), Jung would devote a considerable amount of time to analyzing the symbol of the fish in relation to the development of Christianity. He relates that, while working on *Aion*, the legend of the quest for the Holy Grail and within it the figure of the Fisher King often came to his mind, and he states that he would unquestionably have had to include the Grail in his studies of alchemy had he not wished to avoid intruding on this field in which his wife was working (1963/1995, p. 241; E. Jung & von Franz, 1970/1980). Once the association with the legend of the Holy Grail is made, several further connections with Jung's anomalous experiences suggest themselves, straddling not just this incident but, arguably, each of the others we have discussed. It is as though a mythic motif and archetypal theme of great importance within Jung's work were shaping his anomalous experiences or finding expression through them.

In bare outline, the legend of the Grail, as summarized by Emma Jung and Marie-Louise von Franz, runs as follows:

> A mysterious, life-preserving and sustenance-dispensing object or vessel [the "Holy Grail"] is guarded by a King [the "Fisher King"] in a castle that is difficult to find. The King is either lame or sick and the surrounding country is devastated. The King can only be restored to health if a knight of conspicuous excellence finds the castle and at the first sight of what he sees there asks a certain question. Should he neglect to put this question, then everything will remain as before, the castle will vanish and the knight will have to set out once more upon the search. Should he finally succeed, after much wandering and many adventures, in finding the Grail Castle again, and should he then ask the question, the King will be restored to health, the land will begin

to grow green, and the hero will become the guardian of the Grail from that time on. (E. Jung & von Franz, 1970/1980, p. 9)

The emergence within Jung's haunting of "The Picture of the Fisherman" evokes the Fisher King of the Grail legend. So too does the previous incident involving the kingfisher. In Jung's initial dream of him, the kingfisher-winged figure Philemon, like the Fisher King, was lame (1963/1995, p. 209). Also clearly evocative is that Jung's walnut table was round, like the Round Table of the Grail legend. In Emma Jung and von Franz's interpretation, the Round Table symbolizes both "the developing consciousness of Christian man in the first millennium" and the "idea of wholeness" and "way towards realization of the Self" (E. Jung & von Franz, 1970/1980, pp. 61, 399).

Some other details are more recondite but easily associated once one looks into the legend. For example, the broken knife evokes the broken sword given to Perceval in Robert de Boron's version of the legend: "One of the requirements of the knight who wins the Grail is that he be able to join [the broken sword] together once more, thus proving that he is the rightful, that is, the foremost and predestined, hero" (E. Jung & von Franz, 1970/1980, p. 81). In Emma Jung and von Franz's interpretation, the sword is broken "through a treacherous misuse, indicating a false application of the intellectual faculties which are therefore no longer capable of functioning in the interests of life ... a failure in the thinking of that age" (pp. 89–90). This interpretation tallies, perhaps not surprisingly, with Jung's view of his own work as, in part, a compensation for the one-sided rationalism of modernity (1957/1970e), which in turn reflects the rationalization and intellectualization associated with disenchantment. Again, even Jung's early anomalous experience of the apparition with detaching heads might be seen in relation to the Grail: In the Welsh version of the Grail legend, "In place of the Grail, a dish is carried in bearing a severed head" (E. Jung & von Franz, 1970/1980, p. 33).

In relation to the episode with Freud, there is no immediate association to the Grail legend, but Jung reports a pertinent dream he had two years later, while working on *The Psychology of the Unconscious*, the book that would make the split between him and Freud inevitable (1963/1995, pp. 186–189; 1911–1912/1919/1991). Two principal figures appeared in the dream: an Imperial Austrian customs official and a medieval knight. Jung was immediately able to relate the customs official to Freud (1963/1995, p. 187). He was, he says, able to get an idea of the meaning of the knight "only much later after I had been meditating on the dream for some time":

> Even in the dream, I knew that that knight belonged to the twelfth century. That was the period when alchemy was beginning and also the quest for the Holy Grail. The stories of the Grail had been of the greatest importance to me ever since I read them, at the age of fifteen, for the first time. I had an inkling that a great secret still lay hidden behind those stories. Therefore it seemed quite natural to me that the dream should conjure up the world of the Knights of the Grail and their quest—for that was, in the deepest sense, my own world,[14] which had scarcely anything to do with Freud's. My whole being was seeking for something still unknown which might confer meaning on the banality of life. (p. 189)

Finally, similarly to the situation with the Grail country, Jung's prophetic visions depicted a land devastated and sterile, and the way to restore it was through a spiritual quest leading to transformation of the individual. Wrote Jung of his realization following the outbreak of World War I: "Now my task was clear: I had to try to understand what had happened [in my visions] and to what extent my own experience coincided with that of mankind in general. Therefore my first obligation was to probe the depths of my own psyche" (p. 200). Here, for Jung, personal meaning and collective meaning seemed to coincide, as he found, or so he believed, an important part of his personal destiny.[15] Among the tasks that this involved was addressing the disenchantment of the modern world and its devastating social, political, and environmental consequences

CONCLUSION

Jung, then, was deeply informed about anomalous phenomena, had wide personal experience of them, and remained boldly engaged with them throughout his long life. Such "synoptic empiricism" (Kelly, 2015, pp. 494, 535) was one of the factors that led him to develop his concept of synchronicity. With this concept, about which he wrote in detail only in his last decade, he offered an approach to understanding anomalous phenomena that remains fully open to them, addresses some of their neglected aspects, in particular their possible personal and collective meaning, and does not shy away from implications of them that challenge mainstream scientific assumptions.

With the concept of synchronicity, Jung affirmed the value of trying to understand anomalous phenomena scientifically, but he proposed an expansion of science in order to do so. The mystery inherent in anomalous phenomena was thus, as it were, enfolded in the concept by which Jung aimed to explain them, in its principle of acausal connection through meaning. As a concept, synchronicity is "antinomial" (Landy & Saler, 2009, pp. 3, 6–7; Saban, 2012, pp. 24–28) or "bimodal" (Josephson–Storm, 2017, pp. 57, 70, 268, 306), being both disenchanting (explaining the anomalous) and (re)enchanting (affirming the anomalous). Synchronicity's enfoldment of the critical consciousness of disenchantment ensures that it does not promote regression to naïve enchantment. But its enfoldment of genuine mystery—"inexplicability" (1952/1969r, para. 967)—equally ensures that it does not promote reductive disenchantment. As we shall see in chapters 3 and 4, synchronicity points toward participative and unitive forms of relationship that cannot be accommodated within mainstream modes of scientific reasoning but require an alternative metaphysical framework.

The concept of synchronicity provides a unified account of a range of seemingly disparate anomalous phenomena and connects them to an overall model of psychology that attends to the whole person. Arguably, synchronicity provides a neater account of some phenomena, such as clairvoyant, telepathic, and precognitive experiences, than of others, such as apparitions, poltergeist activity, and psychokinetic events. But in all cases, it focuses attention on the factor of what the phenomena mean, individually and collectively, and this provides a helpful, complementary perspective to analyses of statistical data and searches for scientific proof and causal explanation.

The meanings that emerged from my tentative analysis of a selection of Jung's anomalous experiences centered on themes of personal transformation, splitting and fragmentation, the restoration of wholeness, and death and reanimation, with the Grail legend as a discernible, if somewhat spectral, narrative emerging within the set of experiences as a whole. Interestingly, this pattern of meanings largely matches what Jung believed was the general social and cultural significance of anomalous phenomena in the present age.

Jung had a view of modernity that tallies closely with that of many 20th-century social theorists (Homans, 1979/1995, pp. 3–8, 135–140, 148–160; Main, 2004, pp. 117–121), and above all, Weber's view of the disenchantment of the world. In sum, Jung saw modernity as a time in which the overvaluation of scientific rationalism had led to a condition of uprootedness, disorientation, meaninglessness, and profound uncertainty (1928/1931/1970d, para. 155; 1934/1969p, para. 815), where in place of a vital religious tradition were found spiritual confusion, loss of myth, and alienation from nature (1933/1934/1970c, para. 313; 1945/1977j, paras. 1360–1368; 1963/1995, pp. 166, 364). In an interview with Mircea Eliade in 1952, Jung expressed this diagnosis of modernity with particular directness and concision, and he added his prescription for a recovery: "The modern world," he stated, "is desacralized, that is why it is in a crisis. Modern man must rediscover a deeper source of his own spiritual life" (McGuire & Hull, 1978, p. 230). Key to this rediscovery, for Jung, was an increased focus on religious experience. But it is interesting to hear, from the same interview, how he understood religious experience and with what he connected it:

> Religious experience is *numinous*, as Rudolf Otto calls it, and for me, as a psychologist, this experience differs from all others in the way it transcends the ordinary categories of space, time, and causality. Recently I have put a great deal of study into

synchronicity (briefly, the "rupture of time"), and I have established that it closely resembles numinous experiences where space, time, and causality are abolished. (p. 230)

It seems that, for Jung, anomalous experiences of the kinds we have been discussing in this chapter—all of which, as Jung stressed, transcend the categories of space, time, and causality—were to be included as forms of numinous or religious experience. Jung's attention to anomalous experiences and his theorization of them in terms of synchronicity could therefore be seen as part of his strategy for rediscovering a deeper source of spirituality in order to resacralize, or reenchant, the modern world and thereby address the crisis of modernity.[16]

ENDNOTES

[1] Strictly speaking, this does not mean that, for Weber, no mysterious, incalculable forces exist, but rather that they are no longer part of the dominant cultural narrative or explanation.

[2] This is not to say that researchers have not considered and even been motivated by the possible implications of anomalous phenomena and the possible applications of whatever mechanisms may underlie them. But these concerns are usually addressed speculatively, as a sketching out of imagined futures (see, for example, Broughton, 1991, pp. 301–366; Radin, 1997, pp. 275–297).

[3] The three book-length studies are "On the Psychology and Pathology of So-Called Occult Phenomena" (1902/1957), "Synchronicity: An Acausal Connecting Principle" (1952/1969r), and "Flying Saucers: A Modern Myth of Things Seen in the Skies" (1958/1970b). Among Jung's shorter papers, see especially Jung (1905/1977m, 1920/1948/1969m, 1934/1969p, 1938/1977e, 1948/1977n, 1950/1977f, 1950–1955/1977i, 1951/1969h, 1954/1977k, 1957/1977d, 1958/1977b, 1960/1977g).

[4] This text must be used with caution in view of the scholarly work that has shown the extent to which hands other than Jung's contributed to its composition and editing (see Elms, 1994; Shamdasani, 1995). However, for most of the incidents recounted here, there are alternative, firsthand, and sometimes more nearly contemporaneous sources in Jung (1990; 1973a; 1976; 2009/2012; 2020). Versions of the present summaries of the incidents have appeared previously in Main (1997, pp. 2–6; 2004, pp. 66-70).

[5] Jung provides the following detail about the picture: "Through the middle of the picture ran a river, and a fisherman with a rod was standing on the shore. He had caught a fish. On the fisherman's head

was a chimney from which flames were leaping and smoke rising. From the other side of the river the devil came flying through the air. He was cursing because his fish had been stolen. But above the fisherman hovered an angel who said, 'You cannot do anything to him; he only catches the bad fish!' My son drew this picture on a Saturday" (1963/1995, p. 215).

6 That Jung could be rigorous in seeking naturalistic explanations for putative paranormal phenomena is shown by his account of a haunting he experienced in England in 1920, in which he draws on the psychology of the unconscious, including the idea of heightened unconscious performance, to account systematically for almost all of the phenomena. See Jung (1950/1977f).

7 For a detailed discussion of the development of the concept of synchronicity in Jung's work and the multiple influences on its formulation, see Main (2004).

8 In the "Résumé" added to the 1955 English edition of his principal synchronicity essay, Jung attempts to refine this tripartite definition in the light of his view that the coinciding events of a synchronicity should both be considered psychic (Jung & Pauli, 1952/1955, pp. 144–145; see also 1952/1969r, para. 855). However, as I have argued in detail elsewhere (2004, pp. 44–47), this attempted refinement generates more problems than it solves, so that the version given here remains the more satisfactory. For further detailed discussion of Jung's definitions, see Main (2004, pp. 12–14, 39–47).

9 Alternative ways of thinking about the difficulty here are that it stems either (1) from the psychic relativity of time and space being necessary but not sufficient conditions for the relativity of mass or (2) from the psychic relativity of time, space, and mass all being aspects of a deeper process.

10 For an alternative classification of anomalous or, as they prefer, "exceptional" experiences, see Atmanspacher and Fach (2013). Their account sees synchronistic experiences as one specific kind of exceptional experience, rather than providing the basis for an overarching explanation. Nevertheless, in the broader metaphysical

framework from which Atmanspacher and Fach's classification derives, namely dual-aspect monism, the principle of synchronicity does play a special role as designating the general correspondence between psychic and physical events seen as epistemic expressions of a unitary underlying ontic domain (see Atmanspacher, 2012, 2021; Atmanspacher & Rickles, 2022).

11 Jung would later write: "Just as the Breuer case ... was decisive for Freud, so a decisive experience underlies my own views. Towards the end of my medical training I observed for a long period a case of somnambulism in a young girl. It became the theme of my doctoral dissertation" (1917/1926/1943/1966a, para. 199).

12 Schiller's expression "the de-divinization [more literally, dis-godding] of Nature" (*die Entgötterung der Natur*), from his poem "The Gods of Greece," is cited as one of the probable influences on Weber's expression "the disenchantment of the world" by, among others, Bishop (2012, p. 57) and Josephson–Storm (2017, pp. 76–89).

13 Two years later, Freud would write, "In matters of occultism I have grown humble since the great lesson Ferenczi's experiences gave me. I promise to believe anything that can be made to seem the least bit reasonable. I shall not do so gladly, that you know. But my hubris has been shattered" (McGuire, 1974, p. 429; Jung, 1963/1995, p. 399).

14 Jung relates that, later, during his travels to India in 1938, a dream about the Grail "Imperiously [...] wiped away all the intense impressions of India and swept me back to the too-long-neglected concerns of the Occident" (1963/1995, pp. 311–313).

15 Synchronicity has previously been associated with the legend of the Holy Grail in Bolen (1982, pp. 99–101) and Main (2007a, pp. 132–140). See also the discussions of Jung's interest in the Grail legend in Kingsley (2018).

16 For further connections between synchronicity and numinosity, see Jung (1947/1954/1969g, para. 405 and note 18; 1952/1969r, paras. 841, 846). For a fuller analysis of the role of synchronicity in Jung's critique of modernity, see Main (2004, pp. 117–143).

3
Meaning

One important concomitant of the historical process of disenchantment, as the Canadian philosopher and social theorist Charles Taylor (2007, pp. 29–35) has elaborated, is a transformation of the way in which meaning is experienced. In the enchanted, premodern world, according to Taylor, meaning was experienced as residing not only in human minds but also in nonhuman subjects and in things (pp. 31–33). In this world, objects could be "charged," "magical"; they could "impose meanings and bring about physical outcomes proportionate to their meanings"; they had "influence and causal power" (p. 35). Meaning was an inherent feature of the world. In the disenchanted, modern world, by contrast, meaning resides exclusively in the inward space of human minds (pp. 30–31), objects are not "charged," and "the causal relations between things cannot be in any way dependent on their meanings, which must be projected on them from our minds" (p. 35). Meaning is no longer experienced as an inherent feature of the world.

For Max Weber (1919/1948d), this transformation in the experience of meaning had implications for the understanding of both meaning *in* science and the meaning *of* science. Since in the disenchanted worldview meaning is entirely mind-dependent, science, conceived of as dealing with mind-independent external realities, has nothing to say about meaning. Science can tell us about facts but not about values or meanings. Egil Asprem (2014) calls this perspective "axiological scepticism" (pp. 35–37). Of course, empirical psychology can establish the fact that people do ascribe meaning and that they have different "meaning systems" (Paloutzian & Park, 2013, pp. 11–14) for doing so. Such approaches can reveal much that is important about how we "make meaning" (pp. 11–12). But they do not establish meaning as an inherent feature of reality, rather than as a construction, nor therefore can they provide an ontological grounding for any specific ascription of meaning.

Of particular concern to Weber (1919/1948d) was that, since science can tell us nothing about values or meanings, it cannot establish the meaning or value of science itself. Weber made this latter point with especial vividness when he reflected on "the vocation of science within the total life of humanity" (p. 140). He noted Leo Tolstoy's (1828–1910) judgment that, with its emphasis on endless progress, science has rendered death, and hence also civilized life, meaningless because now "civilized man ... catches only the most minute part of what the life of the spirit brings forth ever anew, and what he seizes is always something provisional and not definitive" (p. 140). As we saw in Chapter 1, Weber considered any claims that science was able to reveal ultimate truths or meanings—as had been believed by Plato, Leonardo, Galileo, Bacon, and thinkers influenced by Puritanism—to be "illusions" that had now been dispelled (pp. 140–143).

This is not to say that science lacked meaning and value for Weber, but such meaning and value stemmed from extra-scientific commitments. Weber himself judged science to be "an objectively valuable 'vocation'" (p. 152), not only for its practical utility (pp. 144–145) and generation of specialist knowledge that is "important in the sense that it is 'worth being known'" (p. 143) but also, and more fundamentally, for its "methods of thinking" (p. 150) and ability to bring about "self-clarification and a sense of responsibility" (p. 152). But he was forced to acknowledge that such meanings are based on presuppositions that themselves "cannot be proved by scientific means" but must be rejected or accepted "according to our ultimate position towards life" (p. 143; see also p. 153), that is, according to our preferences.

Since science, despite its spectacular explanatory successes, is unable to discern any meaning in the physical world, the physical world appears to be fundamentally devoid of meaning. And since, in dominant versions of the disenchanted worldview, life and consciousness are deemed to be epiphenomena of physical processes, they too, in all their manifold expressions, are also ultimately devoid of meaning (see Russell, 1903/2013, p. 231). Indeed, the experience of meaning itself, in this view, is an epiphenomenon of physical processes in the brain, from where, as Taylor notes, it is then projected onto the world.

This is an extraordinary and profoundly counterintuitive view of reality, and one with serious practical consequences. For, as critics of disenchantment point out, if the world is ultimately devoid of meaning beyond that which human subjects delusively project onto it, it is difficult to develop compelling arguments against the kind of predatory and exploitative relationships toward the world—the natural environment, other cultures, societies, individuals, and even ourselves—that are so widespread today as well as in the historical record (Bilgrami, 2010, pp. 148–152).[1]

This grim assessment of the impact of the intellectualist rationalization of disenchantment on modern experiences of meaning was broadly shared by both Jung and one of Jung's most important scientific interlocutors, the physicist Wolfgang Pauli. For Jung, as he states in his late essay "The Undiscovered Self: Present and Future" (1957/1970e), science, by which he means the dominant scientific rationalism, "is based in the main on statistical truths and abstract knowledge and therefore imparts an unrealistic, rational picture of the world" (para. 498). This, he argues, leads to a "levelling down" of "not only the psyche but the individual man and, indeed, all individual events whatsoever" (para. 499). The "statistical world-picture," he continues, thus "thrusts aside the individual in favour of anonymous units that pile up into mass formations"—"organizations," "the abstract idea of the State"—which submerge "The goal and meaning of individual life (which is the only *real* life)" (para. 499). The consequences of such "psychological mass-mindedness" (para. 501) brought about by scientific rationalism show up, in Jung's view, both in individual pathology, where one-sidedly intellectual patients cut off from their instincts and emotions suffer a sense of "meaninglessness" (1934/1969p, para. 815; cf. 1951/1969h, para. 982; 1952/1969r, para. 845), and in the social and political sphere where, he argues, mass-mindedness provides the conditions in which totalitarianism can flourish (1957/1970e, paras. 488–516; see also Main, 2004, pp. 117–121, 135–138).

Pauli (1952/1955), too, as a natural rather than social scientist, was concerned about both the personal and collective consequences of the one-sided "rationalistic attitude of scientists since the eighteenth century" (p. 153) and the accompanying "de-animation of the physical world" (p. 156). While he greatly valued the knowledge that could be gained through science, the role of science in improving living conditions, and the personal satisfaction of achieving scientific insight (p. 152; see also Gieser, 2005, p. 258), he felt that current science, which for him meant in particular physics, was incomplete because of its exclusion of feeling, value, psychological reality, and the realm of the nonrational and qualitative generally (see, e.g., Pauli, 1952/1955, pp. 206–208; Meier, 2001, pp. 195–196; Gieser, 2005, p. 140). At the individual level, this exclusion fostered a hypertrophy of reason such as, in his own case, had precipitated the personal crisis that led to his seeking treatment from Jung (Gieser, 2005, pp. 142–154; Miller, 2009, pp. 124–147). At a more social and political level, scientific rationalism resulted in a perilous dissociation of science from morality—a situation epitomized for Pauli by the direct and indirect involvement of physicists in the development of the atom bomb and their complicity thereby in mass murder (Gieser, 2005, pp. 23, 323–324; Miller, 2009, p. 176).

While Weber believed that the science-driven rationalization and disenchantment of the modern Western world were an inevitability to which we would have to reconcile ourselves, Jung and Pauli believed that these processes might be tempered, if not in important respects reversed, by the development of a revised understanding of science—an understanding that somehow would reconnect science with excluded aspects of meaning in a fundamental way. The specific proposal for how this might be done was the concept of synchronicity, developed by Jung (1952/1969r) with substantive contributions and much critical encouragement from Pauli (1952/1955; Meier, 2001). As we saw in Chapter 1, Jung's overall response to disenchantment was to develop the process of individuation, but within individuation the crucial moments of transformation from disenchantment to reenchantment are specifically bound up with the concept of synchronicity.

With the concept of synchronicity, Jung proposed, as described in Chapter 2, that events not otherwise related to one another by efficient causation can be connected through the meaning they jointly express, through standing in a relationship of "meaningful coincidence" (1952/1969r, para. 827) or, as Pauli preferred, "meaning-correspondence" (Meier, 2001, p. 44). In the present chapter, I ask both what Jung means by "meaning" in relation to synchronicity and how, in his view, this understanding of meaning might help with the problem of the seemingly negative, "disenchanting" impact of scientific rationalism on modern experiences of meaning.

THE MEANING OF "MEANING" IN "MEANINGFUL COINCIDENCE"

Jung himself does not present a systematic account of meaning in synchronicity, nor does there appear to be a clear consensus about Jung's understanding of meaning among subsequent Jungian writers, whether they focus on synchronicity or discuss analytical psychology more generally (Jaffé, 1970; Mathers, 2001; Giegerich, 2004; Kime, 2019; Atmanspacher & Rickles, 2022). This lack of consensus is evident from an exchange that took place in the pages of the *Journal of Analytical Psychology* between 2011 and 2012, in which two prominent Jungians, Warren Colman and Wolfgang Giegerich, offered views about meaning in synchronicity that diverge radically not only from each other but also from Jung's own primary focus (see Colman, 2011, 2012; Giegerich, 2012). I shall briefly summarize their debate as it highlights a number of important issues and provides a useful point of entry into the topic of the present chapter.

Constructed, Quasi-Linguistic, or Cosmic?

In his initial paper Colman (2011) argues that, with his concept of synchronicity, Jung was trying to establish scientifically an objective principle of meaning in nature, a meaning that, as Jung puts it, "is *a priori* in relation to human consciousness and apparently exists outside man" (1952/1969r, para. 942). Colman (2011) sees this as tantamount to Jung's trying to establish the reality of "the Self ... as ... a Greater Subject," the "Universal Mind," or "In short, God" (p. 472; see also pp. 481–482). Colman himself proposes "the contrary view that the meaning in synchronicity is a function of human meaning-making ... a phenomenon of human being in the world in which meaning is generated out of the interaction *between* mind and Nature" (p. 472). He presents a sophisticated account of such meaning-making in terms of events being associated not causally and logically, as in science, but through congruent correspondence, as in primordial thinking and poetic metaphor, and their then being retroactively organized into narratives (pp. 480–487).

In a challenging response, Giegerich (2012) takes issue with Colman's, and other authors' (e.g., Hogenson, 2005, 2009), focus on the impact that synchronistic events may have subjectively on experiencers or the role they can play in terms of human meaning-making. Giegerich (2012) sees this focus as stemming from a misunderstanding of the German word translated into English as "meaningful" in the phrase "meaningful coincidence" (*sinngemäße Koinzidenz*):

> The difference between *sinnvoll* and *sinngemäß* is crucial. When one reports what someone else said, adding that the report will be *sinngemäß*, one indicates that what follows is not a verbatim quotation, but merely "roughly the same," a repetition "faithful to" (*gemäß*) the basic *Sinn* (intended meaning) of what had been said, but now presented in the present speaker's own words or summary, as it were the speaker's version of the gist of it. Whether what you cite in a *sinngemäß* way also happens to be *sinnvoll* (meaningful) or not is another question entirely. (p. 502)

In Giegerich's (2012) reading, what Jung means in calling an event a "meaningful coincidence" is merely that "the inner and outer event [of the coincidence] 'mean roughly the same thing'" (p. 502). This use of meaning, he stresses, is "quite sober, down to earth, close to 'concept' or 'notion' ...

roughly the same as when we speak of the meaning of a word" and "has absolutely nothing to do with Meaning with a capital M, with human *experiences* of meaning, with what is meaningful *for us* and makes existence meaningful, let alone with transcendent meaning" (p. 502). The impact of a synchronicity, such as the way the famous event with the scarab beetle allegedly had a positive effect on Jung's analysis of his patient, is to be seen merely as an "after-effect," "an additional piece of information about the serendipitous subsequent course of events and remains external to the synchronicity event itself" (p. 506). For Giegerich, Jung's aim with his concept of synchronicity was to address not the subjective interpretation of events but "an extremely puzzling, intellectually challenging *objective* problem: the problem given with the *events* themselves"; it is "a strictly intellectual problem, a challenge for the scientific mind. And the solution offered by Jung is also a rational one" (p. 505).

In his reply to Giegerich, Colman (2012) notes that there are fluent German speakers, including Marie-Louise von Franz, the first main successor to Jung's work on synchronicity, who apparently do not share Giegerich's (2012, p. 503) exclusively "low-key, quasi-linguistic" under-standing of the phrase *sinngemäße Koinzidenz*. So the issue may be one of different interpretations rather than of mistranslation (Colman, 2012, p. 513; see, e.g., von Franz, 1992, p. 258). Colman (2012) also notes that the notion of rough correspondence, which Giegerich attributes to Jung, makes it virtually impossible to distinguish "where coincidence ends and synchronicity begins or *vice versa*" (p. 513). There is a need for a factor beyond just rough correspondence that converts a mere coincidence into a meaningful coincidence. For Jung, Colman (2012, pp. 513–514) observes, this is the connection of synchronicity to archetypes with their "highly numinous symbolic images" and "psychoid" nature, which point precisely to a kind of "'cosmic' meaning" and "Grand Narrative." Colman himself, however, remains "unpersuaded by any non-psychic explanation" of archetypes in terms of "self-subsistent meaning" and concludes by reaffirming his claim "that the meaning-making psyche is inextricably involved in the significant correlations of *sinngemäße Koinzidenz*" (p. 516).

Despite the differences between Colman and Giegerich, they also have a notable area of agreement in their shared criticism of Jungian interest in the *unus mundus* (the idea of an underlying unitary reality) and the possibility that synchronicity may provide "an opening to the sacred and to transcendence" (Giegerich, 2012, p. 505; Colman, 2012, pp. 512–513). Both steer away from accepting any transcendental, cosmic, or religious interpretation of the meaning involved in synchronicities. Colman finds such an interpretation in Jung but rejects it. Giegerich denies that it exists in Jung's work on synchronicity, which he considers to be an exclusively scientific project.

In what follows I shall argue that the objective, transcendental interpretation of meaning is indeed present in Jung's work on synchronicity and that this can most accurately and also most helpfully be viewed as coexisting with, rather than being an alternative to, interpretations of synchronistic meaning in terms of either parallel content (à la Giegerich) or subjective effect and meaning-making (à la Colman). In his work on synchronicity, Jung's primary focus was indeed on science, but far from being unconcerned with psychological and ultimately spiritual matters, his aim was to propose a revision of our understanding of science that would cease to exclude these from its world picture. The tensions between the understandings of Colman and Giegerich, and the divergence of both from Jung's position, can be lessened by recognizing that Jung implicitly referred to several levels of meaning in his work on synchronicity and that all these levels are underpinned by the concept of the archetype understood as "psychoid."

Levels of Meaning

Robert Aziz (1990), in his close examination of the concept of synchronicity in relation to Jung's psychology of religion, identified "four interrelated layers of meaning" involved in synchronistic experiences (pp. 64–66, 75–84). The first of these levels is simply the fact of two or more events paralleling one another. The paralleling is by virtue of a shared content or meaning, such as Jung's patient's dream and the appearance of the insect at Jung's consulting room window involving the same or very similar content of a scarab or scarabaeid beetle. This understanding of meaning is expressed many times in Jung's principal essay on synchronicity (1952/1969r). For example, he refers to images standing "in an analogous or equivalent (i.e., meaningful) relationship to objective occurrences" (para. 856) and to "the simultaneous occurrence of a psychic state with a physical process as an *equivalence of* meaning" (para. 865). This is the level of meaning that Giegerich stresses.

The second level of meaning identified by Aziz consists of the emotional charge or "numinosity" attending synchronistic events. Jung (1952/1969r) notes the "important role" that "the emotional factor" plays in synchronicities (para. 846), which indeed are sometimes experienced as being "dependent on affects" (para. 860). This emotional charge is a source of nonrational or prereflective meaning, suggested in Jung's example by the way in which, when the synchronicity occurred, his patient's "natural being could burst through the armor of her animus possession" (para. 845). This level of meaning complements and destabilizes the first level, evoking beneath the rationally graspable paralleling of content between the psychic and physical events a dimension of deep emotionality, otherness, and ambiguity. Colman (2011) seems to acknowledge this level when he writes of synchronistic experiences producing "an uncanny sense of what I can best describe as a feeling that the universe is alive" (p. 475; see also 2012, p. 514).

Aziz's third level of meaning is the significance of the synchronicity interpreted subjectively, from the point of view of the experiencers' personal developmental needs and goals, unconscious as well as conscious—in Jungian terms, their individuation. Although Jung, rather surprisingly for a psychotherapist, does not write much about this level of meaning in synchronicities, it is suggested by his comment (1952/1969r, para. 816) regarding "how much these inner experiences [viz. synchronicities] meant to my patients." More specifically, in his famous example, it is expressed by the way in which, following the synchronistic event and presumably also Jung's and the patient's attempts to understand it and relate it to the patient's situation, "the [patient's] process of transformation could at last begin to move" (para. 845) and "The treatment could now be continued with satisfactory results" (1951/1969h, para. 982). This is the kind of meaning with which Colman and many other analysts who write about synchronicity seem to be primarily concerned, but which Giegerich considers to be an "after-effect ... external to the synchronicity event itself."

The fourth and last of the levels of meaning identified by Aziz is the significance of the synchronicity objectively, that is, as the expression of archetypal meaning that is transcendental to human consciousness. As Jung (1952/1969r) states explicitly, "Synchronicity postulates a meaning which is *a priori* in relation to human consciousness and apparently exists outside man" (para. 942). From the symbolism of his example, he infers that the objective, transcendental meaning involved was that of the archetype of rebirth, since "The scarab is a classic example of a rebirth symbol" (para. 845). It is the postulation of this kind of objective meaning that most radically challenges the perspective of disenchantment, for disenchantment, as we have seen, implies that there is no such objective meaning, or at any rate none that can receive support from the findings of science. Giegerich and Colman both seem to be skeptical about this level of objective, transcendental meaning.

The existence of levels of meaning of the kind discussed above is not idiosyncratic to Jungian thought. As the psychologist Roy Baumeister observes in his interdisciplinary study *Meanings of Life* (1991), depth psychologists, literary critics, and even diplomats frequently recognize different levels of meaning (p. 20). When they do so, what the levels usually refer to is, roughly, "the quantity and complexity of the relationships that are subsumed":

> the simplest uses of meaning associate labels (such as names) to specific, immediate objects. These uses of meaning tend to be concrete and to be limited in time. In contrast, the highest levels of meaning may refer to complex, far-reaching relationships that transcend the immediate situation and may even approach timeless or eternal perspectives. ... In an important sense, higher level meanings refer to contexts for lower levels. (pp. 20-21)

What interrelates the four levels of meaning identified by Aziz is the concept of the archetype. For while Aziz (1990) calls the fourth, objective level of meaning the "archetypal level" (p. 66), each of his other three levels of meaning also depends on the presence of the archetype. The shared meaning by virtue of which two or more events are taken to have parallel content and so to be in a synchronistic relationship derives from an archetype: for example, in Jung's paradigmatic synchronicity, underlying the scarab symbol in both its psychic and its physical appearances is the archetype of rebirth (1952/1969r, para. 845). The numinous charge that Jung finds associated with synchronicities is something that, he argues, stems from the presence of an activated archetype (para. 841). And insofar as the subjective level of meaning is evaluated with reference to the developmental process of individuation, this too will also be based on archetypes, since the activation of archetypes—shadow, animus/anima, self—is intrinsic to individuation for Jung (1928/1966d, paras. 266–406; 1951/1968b, paras. 1–67). This identification of archetypes as providing the basis of synchronicity is in fact explicitly made by Jung: "by far the greatest number of synchronistic phenomena that I have had occasion to observe and analyze," he writes, "can easily be shown to have a direct connection with the archetype" (1952/1969r, para. 912; see also paras. 845–846; 1976, pp. 437, 447, 490). Consistently with Baumeister's observation, Aziz's fourth, archetypal level of meaning in synchronicity can be seen both as the highest level and as providing the context for the other levels.[2]

The Archetype as Psychoid

In his synchronicity essay, Jung (1952/1969r) writes that archetypes "constitute the structure of the collective unconscious" (para. 840), that they are "formal factors responsible for the organization of unconscious psychic processes: they are 'patterns of behaviour,'" and that "they have a 'specific charge' and develop numinous effects which express themselves as *affects*" (para. 841). This is all consonant with what Jung had been writing for years. But in the synchronicity essay, he articulates some novel characteristics that reveal archetypes to be not just psychic but what he calls "psychoid" factors. In characterizing archetypes as "psychoid," he means that they cannot be fully represented psychically and therefore cannot simply be equated with "perceptible psychic phenomena" (para. 840). At an irrepresentable level, he suggests, archetypes can structure matter as well as psyche—and not just separately but at the same time in respect to the same pattern of meaning. Thus, of archetypes as "psychoid factors" he writes:[3]

> These are *indefinite*, that is to say they can be known and determined only approximately. Although associated with causal processes, or "carried" by them, they continually go beyond their frame of reference, an infringement to which I would give the name "transgressivity," because the archetypes are not found exclusively in the psychic sphere, but can occur just as much in circumstances that are not psychic (equivalence of an outward physical process with a psychic one). (para. 964)

For Jung, the psychoid nature of archetypes is most clearly evinced by number archetypes. In the synchronicity essay itself, this is largely left implicit. Jung highlights the archetypal character of natural numbers (para. 870), but he primarily focuses on the psychic properties of number archetypes and their role in divination procedures (paras. 863–870). However, in a subsequent letter to Pauli (24 October 1953), he is more explicit about the broader significance of number archetypes as the paradigmatic psychoid factors. As "the simplest and most elementary of all archetypes," he writes, number archetypes can help "to locate and describe that region which is indisputably common to both [physics and psychology]" (Meier, 2001, p. 127). For numbers "possess that characteristic of the psychoid archetype in classical form—namely, that *they are as much inside as outside*" (p. 127). This, Jung suggests, is why "equations can be devised from purely mathematical prerequisites" and these equations later "will turn out to be formulations of physical processes" (p. 127). He thus concludes that "from the psychological point of view at least, the sought-after borderland between physics and psychology lies in the secret of the number" (p. 127).[3]

In his essay, Jung (1952/1969r) also characterizes archetypes as representing "psychic probability" (para. 964). This formulation highlights another analogy between physics and Jung's depth psychology, thereby again enhancing the plausibility of connecting the two. As Jung neatly summarized it in a letter to Pauli (13 January 1951): "In physical terms, probability corresponds to the so-called law of nature; psychically, it corresponds to the archetype" (Meier, 2001, p. 70).

These developments in Jung's thinking about archetypes, each of which facilitates a rapprochement between psychology and physics, were all prompted by Pauli's criticisms of earlier drafts of Jung's essay. Pauli was concerned in particular about Jung's placing discontinuous phenomena in physics on the same level as synchronicity, since, as Pauli explained, "microphysics ... has no use for the concept of 'meaning'" (Meier, 2001, p. 56)—except to the minimal extent that "The term 'state' or 'physical situation' in quantum physics" might be "a preliminary stage for [the] more general term 'meaningful connection'" (p. 56n5). To allow for the "broader definition" of synchronicity that encompasses acausal phenomena in microphysics—the definition that Jung and eventually Pauli both favored (pp. 59–62, 63–65)—it was necessary for the concept of the archetype, which was currently "inadequate" for this purpose, to undergo change (p. 65). Hence its reformulation as "psychoid" and as representing "psychic probability"—and Pauli suspected that "more changes are in the offing" (p. 65).[4]

Meaning in Synchronicity

Having clarified that for Jung the meaning in synchronicities is multileveled and is underpinned at all levels by the concept of the psychoid archetype, I should now like to return to the debate between Colman and Giegerich and offer a few comments on their respective positions. First, I think Giegerich is right to emphasize that the first of the four levels of meaning identified by Aziz, paralleling of content, is of much greater concern to Jung in "Synchronicity: An Acausal Connecting Principle" (and indeed in most of the other places where he discusses synchronicity) than is the third, subjective level of meaning, which Colman emphasizes. In the essay, there are many references to meaning at the level of parallel content, several of them receiving italicized emphasis by Jung. In addition to the examples mentioned earlier, Jung (1952/1969r) refers to "meaningful coincidence" and "a kind of *meaningful cross-connection*" (para. 827; emphasis in original); to how "the connecting principle [in synchronicities] must lie in the *equal significance* of the parallel events; in other words, their *tertium comparationis* [the third element of comparison] is *meaning*" (para. 915; emphasis in original); and to a "factor in nature which expresses itself in the arrangement of events and appears to us as meaning" (para. 962). In contrast, there are no explicit references to the subjective level of meaning apart from Jung's briefly recalling in the "Foreword" of the essay "how much these inner experiences meant to my patients" (para. 816) and (*pace* Giegerich) his recounting of the incident involving the scarab beetle, which, even with its scarcity of "relevant subjective information" (Aziz, 1990, p. 65), does provide an outline of how the synchronicity fostered the patient's "process of transformation" (Jung, 1952/1969r, para. 845; cf. 1951/1969h, para. 982).

Giegerich is also clearly right that in his writing on synchronicity, Jung is more immediately concerned with science than therapy. The synchronicity essay begins and ends with discussions of subatomic physics and issues in the philosophy of science (Jung, 1952/1969r, paras. 818–820, 959–968), and in between there are various forays into parapsychology (paras. 833–840) and descriptive biology (paras. 821–822). By contrast, such references as there are to the therapeutic implications of synchronicity are brief and primarily illustrative (paras. 843–845). Even outside of the essay it is surprisingly difficult to find places where Jung does discuss the subjective or therapeutic effects of synchronicity (see Main, 2007b, pp. 360, 362–364).

However, Giegerich seems to overplay this hand. Even if Jung does not evince much concern with Aziz's third, subjective level of meaning, there is plenty of evidence of his concern with the fourth, objective level. In fact, the greatest number of explicit references to meaning in Jung's essay concerns the objective or archetypal level. He refers (1952/1969r) to meaning that is "*a priori* in relation to human consciousness" (para. 942), "self-subsistent" (para. 944), "transcendental" (para. 915), and can "exist outside the psyche" (para. 915). He also devotes many pages to setting out some of the considerations that, for him, point to the existence of objective meaning. Chief among these considerations are synchronistic phenomena themselves, whether spontaneous or induced, with their apparent ability to transcend the limitations of space and time to reveal "'absolute knowledge' ... a knowledge not mediated by the sense organs ..., knowledge of future or spatially distant events" (para. 948). In addition, by way of cultural support, Jung adduces in Chapter 3 of the essay a range of Chinese, Greek, medieval, and Renaissance forerunners of his idea of synchronicity—notions of Tao, the sympathy of all things, correspondences, microcosm and macrocosm, and preestablished harmony—each of which presupposes the existence of objective meaning (paras. 916–946).

As further indications of objective meaning, Jung refers to dreams whose content, involving "the meaningful coincidence of an absolutely natural product with a human idea apparently independent of it," seems to suggest the notion of self-subsistent meaning (paras. 945–946). He cites the "'meaningful' or 'intelligent' behaviour of the lower organisms, which are without a brain" (pars. 947–948). And he also notes out-of-body experiences or, as he refers to them, "remarkable observations made during deep syncopes" (pars. 949–955). In the light of all this counter-evidence, it is clearly not the case that Jung is exclusively preoccupied in the essay with the level of simple paralleling of content. Furthermore, while Jung may have been primarily engaged with a scientific problem, the nature of this problem was precisely how to revise science in such a way as to open it up to include psychological and indeed spiritual factors—in particular, factors associated with the concept of the archetype (para. 962).

When Giegerich (2012, p. 502) writes that Jung's "low-key, quasi-linguistic" use of meaning "has absolutely nothing to do with Meaning with a capital M, with human *experiences* of meaning, with what is meaningful *for* us and makes existence meaningful, let alone with transcendent meaning," he seems to suggest that the quasi-linguistic level of meaning is of such a radically different kind as to preclude connection with the higher levels of meaning he enumerates. Yet this is not necessarily so. As Baumeister (1991) notes:

> The meaning of a life is the same kind of meaning as the meaning of a sentence in several important respects: having the parts fit together into a coherent pattern, being capable of being understood by others, fitting into a broader context, and invoking implicit assumptions shared by other members of the culture. ... Meanings of life are a special usage of meaning, not a special kind of meaning. (p. 16)

For Jung, too, as suggested above, there is continuity among levels of meaning. On the one hand, he claims that archetypes, when their motifs are culturally elaborated into myths, can help us to "frame a view of the world which adequately explains the meaning of human existence in the cosmos" (1963/1995, p. 373). On the other hand, he notes that all interpretations "make use of certain linguistic matrices that are themselves derived from primordial images [i.e., archetypes]" (1934/1954/1968a, para. 67). For Jung, the archetype provides the "source" (para. 67) of both the cosmic and the linguistic meaning. He refers to the "equivalences" in synchronistic events—the equivalences that Giegerich finds so "sober" and "down to earth" (2012, p. 502)—as "*archetypal* equivalences" (Jung, 1952/1969r, para. 964; emphasis added). In view of the more transcendental directions in which Jung goes elsewhere in his essay, it would seem that his low-key, quasi-linguistic uses of meaning are intended to facilitate its discussion at the most basic level in relation to problems of science. Having done this, he can then show—or imply and leave for others to show—how, through the concept of the archetype, this entails the inclusion of richer and more complex levels of meaning as well. His approach also facilitates understanding of how coincidences, whose content—such as the appearance and behavior of a beetle—might at the basic level of paralleling seem trivial, can readily open into deeper levels of numinous, transformational, and transpersonal meaning, especially when interpreted with sensitivity to symbolism.[5]

Colman (2012), for his part, in his reply to Giegerich, seems to me right to argue that if the meaning in synchronicity referred to nothing more than "rough correspondence," we would have no way of distinguishing meaningful from mere coincidences (p. 513). For even series of events that Jung in the end judges not to be synchronistic, such as a run of experiences he mentions involving fishes (see 1952/1969r, paras. 826–827; 1951/1969h, paras. 969–971), do have roughly corresponding, parallel content. Colman is also, I think, clearly right that the factor which for Jung enables this distinction to be made between meaningful and mere coincidences is the archetype understood as numinous and psychoid.

Colman's overall assessment, in his original paper, of Jung's aim as being to establish scientifically an objective principle of meaning in nature, with far-reaching religious implications, also seems to me correct and is well supported by the evidence in the essay itself, as we have seen. That Jung's concern with objective meaning might indeed lead him into religious territory, as Colman suggests, is indicated by, for example, Jung's (1952/1969r) willingness, following Richard Wilhelm, to equate the kind of meaning he has in mind with Tao, "one of the oldest and most central ideas [in Chinese philosophy], which the Jesuits translated as 'God'" (para. 917; cf. 1935/1977r, para. 143).

While recognizing this focus of Jung's, Colman himself develops implications of synchronicity at Aziz's third level of subjective meaning. Despite Jung's own lack of attention to this level, developing it is, as we have seen, not inconsistent with what Jung wrote in his synchronicity essay; and outside the essay, there are other cases, albeit not many and not very detailed, where Jung interpreted synchronistic events in relation to the experiencer's subjective or therapeutic concerns (Main, 2007b, pp. 362–364). But perhaps most telling is that when this aspect of synchronicity was picked up by other analysts, Jung was quick to approve. For example, Michael Fordham, in his book chapter "Reflections on the Archetypes and Synchronicity" (1957), discusses in some detail the therapeutic aspects of both Jung's scarab incident and a synchronicity from his own clinical experience (pp. 42–50). Jung read this in manuscript and praised it in a letter to Fordham (3 January 1957) as "the most intelligent thing that has been said hitherto about this remote subject" (1976, pp. 343–344). From this it is clear that Jung did recognize the subjective, psychological, meaning-making aspect of synchronicity and affirmed the value of exploring it.

There thus seems to be a misplaced emphasis when Colman (2011) writes that he is presenting "the *contrary view* that the meaning in synchronicity is a function of human meaning-making" (p. 472; emphasis added). Jung is acutely aware of the human contribution to the emergence of meaning and struggles with this awareness when attempting to make his case for the existence also of objective meaning. He acknowledges that, as usually understood, "meaning is an anthropomorphic interpretation" (1952/1969r, para. 916); that "What that factor which appears to us as 'meaning' may be in itself we have no possibility of knowing" (ibid.); and specifically that "we have absolutely no scientific means of proving the existence of an *objective* meaning which is not just a psychic product" (para. 915)—not least since, as he would later write to Erich Neumann (10 March 1959), "Meaningfulness always appears to be unconscious at first, and can therefore only be discovered *post hoc*; hence there is always the danger that meaning will be read into things where actually there is nothing of the sort" (1976, p. 495).

If, despite his recognition of these difficulties, Jung continues to argue for the existence of objective meaning, this is not to the detriment of the subjective level of meaning. For Jung, the transcendental view of meaning is not incompatible with a view that sees meaning as "a phenomenon of human being in the world" involving "the interaction *between* mind and Nature" (Colman, 2011, p. 472). As Aziz (1990) and Victor Mansfield (1995, 2002) have elaborated, in synchronistic experiences—as in individuation generally—transcendental, archetypal meaning can enter the lives of individuals through the dynamic of unconscious compensation of their conscious attitude. The meaning expresses itself through archetypal imagery inflected by the experiencers' circumstances and, if integrated, promotes the experiencers' individuation (Aziz, 1990, pp. 80–84; Mansfield, 1995, pp. 16–19; 2002, pp. 124–128). But it also remains transcendental. In other words, the objective meaning can be carried by the subjective, transformational processes of an individual, as in the case of Jung's patient, whose personal "rebirth" was arguably an instance of a more collective process that, as archetypal, is, as it were, cosmically inscribed and indeed may also, Jung hinted, simultaneously have been manifesting itself at a cultural level, as the expression of a needed "rebirth" within Western culture (Main, 2013b, pp. 134–144).

Even more important, however, is that the concept of synchronicity itself breaks down, or at least renders ambiguous, the relationship between subjective and objective meaning. As Jung (1952/1969r) remarks in the final chapter of his essay, synchronicity shows the possibility of "getting rid of the incommensurability between the observed and the observer" and thereby bringing about a "unity of being" (para. 960). This leads to a much more participatory relationship, in which the subject or self is not separate from the object or world and in which, moreover, both self and world are liable to be transformed. Such participatory consciousness, in which human subjectivity is recognized as part of the world's objectivity—even, as Richard Tarnas puts it, as "the organ of the world's own process of self-revelation" (1991/1996, p. 434)—has often been touted as the kernel of the needed response to disenchantment (Berman, 1981, pp. 135–152; Tarnas, 1991/1996, pp. 433–440; Brown, 2020, pp. 161–189). Among other things, such a unity of being, with its implied interconnectedness between the self and the world, would likely lead to more salubrious, cooperative relations between humans and nature, among humans, and even toward ourselves than does the divided, competitive state fostered by dis-enchantment.

As we shall see more fully in Chapter 4, Jung's psychology is purposely framed to respect both immanent or material and transcendental or spiritual viewpoints equally, without allowing one to eclipse the other, and this intrinsic doubleness can help to foster productive engagements of analytical psychology both with contemporary social and political problems (Main, 2013a) and with other social theories (Main, 2013c). The wide range of kinds of meaning that can be identified in synchronicity—with their extreme poles, quasi-linguistic and cosmic—may be another expression of this dual secular and religious perspective, and indeed it can be argued that the concept of synchronicity was introduced partly to support this perspective (see Main, 2004, pp. 100–114). Accordingly, to reject the notion of "self-subsistent meaning" and the underpinning "non-psychic," transcendental interpretation of archetypes, as both Giegerich and Colman do, seems to me to risk impoverishing analytical psychology by collapsing one of the deepest cultural tensions held by Jung's thought—the tension between the secular and the religious.

"SHAKING THE SECURITY OF OUR SCIENTIFIC FOUNDATIONS": MEANING IN SCIENCE

In a letter to Richard Hull (24 January 1955) Jung reported: "The latest word about 'Synchronicity' is that it cannot be accepted because it shakes the security of our scientific foundations, *as if this were not exactly the goal I am aiming at*" (1976, p. 217; emphasis added). Pauli, for his part, considered that the final chapter of Jung's main essay on synchronicity might provide "a glimpse into the future of natural philosophy" (Meier, 2001, p. 65). How, then, might synchronicity as a principle of acausal connection through meaning, where meaning is understood to be multileveled and based on the psychoid archetype, shake up and revise the kind of scientific rationalism criticized by Jung and Pauli? And how might synchronicity thereby help with the crisis of meaning in modernity observed by Jung, Pauli, and others, such as Weber with the notion of disenchantment?

Meaning in Matter

Jung (1952/1969r) characterized scientific rationalism—the science that had been ascendant since at least the 17th century—as "triadic," based on the three principles of time, space, and causality. His radical proposal was to introduce synchronicity, and thereby also meaning, as a fourth principle (paras. 961–963; cf. Pauli, 1952/1955, especially pp. 174–175, 204–205, 226–236). This, Jung (1952/1969r) argued, would make possible "a whole judgement" (para. 961) and "a view which includes the psychoid factor [i.e., the archetype] in our description and knowledge of nature—that is, an *a priori* meaning or 'equivalence'" (para. 962).[6]

There are at least three important implications of this proposal. First, the fact that meaning is here recognized as a factor able to connect events that would not otherwise be connected allows for the perception of other sets of relationships than causal relationships. Events that might be disregarded from a causal point of view because they are unique, irrational, creative, or outright anomalous can be grasped from a synchronistic point of view in terms of the patterns of meaning in which they are woven. This in itself undermines the hold of rationalistic science with its exclusive commitment to causal explanation.[7]

The tendency of scientific rationalism to disregard unique and rare events and relationships in favor of the statistical average taxed Jung and provided one of the launching points for his essay (see 1952/1969r, para. 821). In a letter to Fordham (24 January 1955), he bemoaned that "wherever a philosophy based on the sciences prevails . . ., the individual man loses his foothold and becomes 'vermasst,' turned into a mass particle, because as an 'exception' he is valueless" (1976, p. 216). He then asserted that his wish to do something to forestall the perilous social and political consequences of "this blind and dangerous belief in the security of the scientific Trinity [of time, space, and causality]"—above all, the dangers of deindividualization, mass-mindedness, and totalitarianism—was actually "the reason and the motive of my [synchronicity] essay" (p. 216).

Second, Jung's proposal that the archetype is psychoid and can therefore structure or arrange physical as well as psychic events implies that matter is not, as in the disenchanted view of scientific rationalism, fundamentally inert and meaningless—meaning being only something that the human psyche projects onto matter—but rather that matter and its organization can be inherently imbued with meaning. Jung stated this explicitly to Pauli (7 March 1953): "in cases of synchronicity," he wrote, "they [i.e. archetypes] are arrangers of physical circumstances, so that they can also be regarded as a characteristic of Matter (as *the feature that imbues it with meaning*)" (Meier, 2001, p. 101; emphasis added). A clear corollary of this claim, for Jung, was that synchronicity could—at least to some extent (Main, 2011)—contribute to undoing, or transcending, what he described as "the historical process of world despiritualization" (1938/1940/1969n, para. 141), what Pauli called "the de-animation of the physical world" (1952/1955, p. 156), and what Weber most famously termed "the disenchantment of the world" (1919/1948d, p. 155).

Third, because the meaning archetypes imbue is multileveled, ranging from basic levels of ordering, paralleling, and signifying to the kinds of higher levels that inform individual transformation and the framing of meanings of life, the meaning imbuing material circumstances may be as complex as that correlatively imbuing the psyche—which would include religious meaning. This at any rate seems to be implied when Jung, explaining in the same letter to Pauli his reasons for publishing his religious essay "Answer to Job" (1952/1969a) at the same time as his scientific essay "Synchronicity: An Acausal Connecting Principle" (1952/1969r), writes that "by making the assumption [in the synchronicity essay] that 'being is endowed with meaning' (i.e., extension of the archetype in the object)" he was attempting "to open up *a new path to the 'state of spiritualization'* [*Beseeltheit*] *of Matter*" (Meier, 2001, p. 98; emphasis added).[8] The potential implied here for an intimate connection of natural science with psychology and religion opens the prospect for a truly holistic form of understanding.

These were thoughts to which Pauli was broadly receptive. In the letter (27 February 1953) to which Jung was responding, Pauli had written that he now believed in "the possibility of a simultaneous religious and scientific function of the appearance of archetypal symbols" (Meier, 2001, p. 87). In relation to this, he referred (p. 87n5) to the conclusion of his essay on "The Influence of Archetypal Ideas on the Scientific Theories of Kepler" (1952/1955), where he argued that "not only alchemy [as propounded by Robert Fludd (1574–1637)] but the heliocentric idea [as held by Johannes Kepler (1571–1630)]" each proved "the existence of a symbol that had, simultaneously, a religious and a scientific function" (p. 212). In a later letter to Jung (23 December 1953) he wrote of his impression, based on his "physical dream symbolism," that "compensatorily from the unconscious, the tendency is being developed to bring physics much closer to the roots and sources of life, and that what is happening is ultimately *an assimilation of the psychoid archetypes into an extended form of physics*" (Meier, 2001, p. 130; emphasis added). Later again (23 October 1956), he wrote of dreams that seemed to him to be addressing "the problem ... of getting right to the archetypal source of the natural sciences and thus to a new form of religion" (p. 150).[9]

Transformation and "Double Vision"

It is more than incidental that the last two statements of Pauli's draw their content from expressions of the unconscious. From their different disciplinary perspectives, Pauli and Jung were attempting to articulate the basis of a more holistic form of science, one that would include the unconscious as well as consciousness, psyche as well as matter, and the functions of feeling and intuition as well as those of thinking and sensation. But the model they were seeking could not be arrived at simply consciously, outwardly, and intellectually. It also required attention to the unconscious, to the inner world, and to emotions. As Jung asserted (7 March 1953), "only from his wholeness can man create a model of the whole" (Meier, 2001, p. 99). Pauli (27 May 1953) fully agreed with this statement (p. 118), adding with emphasis: "*it is impossible for me to find this* correspondentia *between physics and psychology just through intellectual speculation; it can only properly emerge in the course of the individuation process in the form of accompanying objective statements* [i.e., dreams and fantasies of transpersonal provenance]" (p. 124). At the conclusion of his study of the conflict between the esotericist Fludd, with his qualitative approach to knowledge, and the early modern scientist Kepler, with his new quantitative approach, Pauli (1952/1955) formulated this idea as follows:

> the process of knowing is connected with the religious experience of transmutation undergone by him who acquires knowledge. This connection can only be comprehended through symbols which both imaginatively express the emotional aspect of the experience and stand in vital relationship to the sum total of contemporary knowledge and the actual process of cognition. (p. 212)

Again, this statement has several important implications. One is that scientific insight can be fostered by engaging with symbolic expressions

BREAKING THE SPELL OF DISENCHANTMENT

from the unconscious.[10] Both Jung and Pauli put this implied route to knowledge into practice. In Jung's case, a major source of his psychological insights and theories was his period of imaginative and reflective engagement with his unconscious and its personifications, as recorded in his *Red Book* (2009/2012) and *Black Books* (2020)—the process he would later dub "active imagination" (1947/1954/1969g, para. 403). Notably, he even considered it helpful to posit a specific "archetype of meaning" (1934/1954/1968a, para. 66), which in personified form could be encountered as the image of the Wise Old Man, "the superior master and teacher, the archetype of the spirit, who symbolizes the pre-existent meaning hidden in the chaos of life" (para. 74). This engagement in active imagination, involving transformation of both the conscious and the unconscious psyche, is part of what makes the envisaged knowledge process participative (1955–1956/1970a, paras. 705–706).

Pauli, for his part, attended closely to his dreams, not least when they involved concepts from physics or included figures who seemed to symbolize either a critical attitude toward the prevailing science or the possibility of a new, more holistic science (see Meier, 2001, passim; Gieser, 2005, pp. 180, 319). He also regularly engaged in active imagination (see, e.g., Meier, 2001, pp. 39–40; Pauli, 2002) and even wrote an essay, titled "Modern Examples of 'Background Physics'" (Meier, 2001, pp. 179–196), in which he reflected at length on "the appearance of quantitative terms and concepts from physics in spontaneous fantasies in a qualitative and figurative—i.e., symbolic—sense" (p. 179).

A second point to highlight is Pauli's (1952/1955) statement that the symbols through which the connection between knowing and the religious experience of transformation can be comprehended need to "stand in vital relationship to the sum total of contemporary knowledge" (p. 212). The implication of this is that inner psychological transformation alone will not lead to holistic understanding. As Pauli remarks in his essay on background physics, "*the purely psychological interpretation* only apprehends *half of the matter. The other half is the revealing of the archetypal basis of the terms* actually applied in *modern physics*" (Meier, 2001, p. 180; Pauli's emphasis). For an effective integration of depth psychology with physics, or indeed with any other discipline, the flow of understanding and influence must be two-way, which requires an in-depth and up-to-date knowledge of the discipline in question, in this case physics. As Suzanne Gieser (2005) summarizes, for Pauli "A modern unified vision" of physics and psychology needed to be built "on an equal measure of *introjection* of true knowledge of matter into the psyche, as well as insight into the dynamics of psychic imagery" (p. 258; see also p. 177).[11]

Finally, Jung's and Pauli's view of the relationship between personal transformation and knowledge implies that a fully holistic understanding of the world would only be possible for someone at an advanced stage of individuation. On 23 October 1956, Pauli sent Jung a series of his dreams together with his own commentary. In his reply (December 1956), Jung added interpretations of some of the dreams, including two (dreamed on 1 October 1954 and 26 December 1955) that concerned "the difference between Danish and English" (Meier 2001, p. 143). For Pauli, Danish symbolized everyday language, while English symbolized dream language (p. 146). In the first dream, the difference between the two languages was said to correspond to "the *difference between v and w*" (p. 143; emphasis in original), and Pauli included in his letter a lengthy narration of his attempts to solve the philological conundrum with which his dream had presented him (pp. 143–146). In the second dream, a king told Pauli "with great authority" that he (Pauli) had "an apparatus that enables you to see both Danish and English" (p. 152). Before commenting on the imagery in these dreams, Jung remarked to Pauli that he was "most impressed by your forays into linguistics" (p. 156). He then turned to the symbolism:

> The important thing about the dream of *26 December 1955* is the double vision. This is a distinctive characteristic of the human being who is at one with himself. He sees the inner and outer oppositeness, not just $V = 5$, which is a symbol of the natural person who, with his consciousness based on perception, becomes ensnared in the world of sense perception and its vividness. W (double V), by way of contrast, is the One, *the whole person who, although himself not split, nevertheless perceives both the external*

sensory aspect of the world and also its hidden depths of meaning [emphasis added]. Thus the split is based on the one-sided ensnarement in one or the other aspect. But if man has united the opposites within himself, there is nothing to stop him perceiving both aspects of the world in an objective manner. The inner psychic split is replaced by a split world-picture, and this is inevitable, for without this discrimination, conscious perception would be impossible. It is not in actual fact a split world, for facing the person who is united with himself is an *unus mundus*. He has to split this *one* world in order to be able to perceive it, always bearing in mind that what he is splitting is still the *one* world, and that the split has been predetermined by consciousness. (pp. 156–157)

This is a far-reaching set of statements. Above all, the passage articulates the kind of holistic perspective that Jung believed might result from the inclusion in our scientific picture of the world of a principle of acausal connection through meaning. It points, indeed, beyond participative to unitive states of consciousness. In addition, with its claim that one can perceive "both the external sensory aspect of the world and also its hidden depths of meaning," the passage suggests the dual secular and religious perspective that is arguably intrinsic to analytical psychology (Main, 2013a, 2013c). Again, the references in the passage to an ontological unity ("the *one* world") encountered through an epistemological duality ("a split world-picture") suggest the philosophical position of dual-aspect monism that seems particularly fruitful for understanding Jung's and Pauli's work on synchronicity (Seager, 2009; Atmanspacher, 2012, 2021) and the all-important role of meaning within it (Atmanspacher & Rickles, 2022). Finally, a major part of the argument of this chapter has been that the seemingly low-key, quasi-linguistic usage of "meaning" upon which Jung attempts to build his concept of synchronicity in fact connects, via the concept of the psychoid archetype, with higher levels of meaning reaching all the way up to the most "transcendental" and "cosmic." It therefore seems apt that Jung's far-reaching statements about "the double vision" should emerge here specifically in relation to reflections on linguistics.

CONCLUSION

For the disenchanted perspective articulated by Weber, the world has no inherent meaning, at any rate none for which science—our most successful mode of acquiring knowledge—can provide any support. For many, including Jung and Pauli, this condition of inherent meaninglessness has seemed to be a major cause of serious psychological, social, cultural, political, and environmental problems, above all because it leaves one with no basis for resisting the instrumental, competitive, and predatory relations that characterize so much of modern life.

Contrary to the disenchanted perspective, Jung and Pauli conjectured that there *is* inherent meaning in the world, which informs not just psychic events but also physical occurrences. The key to this conjecture is the shift from viewing archetypes as purely psychic to viewing them as psychoid, that is, as expressions of a psychophysically neutral substrate of empirical reality, what Jung called the *unus mundus* (1955–1956/1970a, paras. 760–761). So understood, archetypes supply, in the apt phrase of Harald Atmanspacher and Dean Rickles (2022), the "deep structure of meaning" (p. xiii).

Synchronistic experiences especially point toward this deep structure of meaning. Through their, as Jung put it, "getting rid of the incommensurability between the observed and the observer" (1952/1969r, para. 960), synchronistic events foster a participatory relationship to reality—suggesting that the reality understood by science is not separate from us or from our psychic activity but is the same reality that we also are. Further, synchronistic experiences provide momentary access to a unitary world (para. 960), the *unus mundus*, and our ultimate identity with it in the *unio mystica* (1955–1956/1970a, paras. 662, 771). In the "double vision" that Jung describes as characteristic of the "whole person," an empirical or dualistic consciousness, attuned to the "external sensory aspect" of the world, is enfolded within a unitive holistic consciousness that can simultaneously perceive the "hidden depths of meaning" of the world (i.e., its objective, archetypal meaning). This reflects how, as we saw in Chapter 1, the dualistic consciousness of disenchantment can be—indeed, needs to be—enfolded within the more unitive consciousness of reenchantment.

ENDNOTES

[1] Of course, there have been many attempts to develop naturalistic and even physicalist accounts of meaning and ethics. But it is far from obvious that they are more successful than the supernaturalist accounts they seek to replace (see, e.g., Seachris, 2013). In the terms used by Joshua Seachris (pp. 10–13), Weber's is a form of nihilism or pessimistic naturalism since the possibility of grounding meaning is denied. Others have proposed forms of optimistic naturalism, affirming that meaning can be grounded, whether objectively or subjectively.

[2] Harald Atmanspacher and Dean Rickles, in their recent book *Dual-Aspect Monism and the Deep Structure of Meaning* (2022), discuss a range of theories of meaning relevant to understanding dual-aspect models of the relationship between mind and matter, such as the model of Jung and Pauli, dubbed "the Pauli–Jung conjecture." These perspectives on meaning can be broadly mapped onto the distinctions I have provided, based on Aziz (1990). Meaning as paralleling of content maps onto meaning as reference, while meaning as numinosity, subjective meaning, and objective meaning all map onto the complex notion of meaning as sense, with its further differentiations as symbolic forms, "stage setting," nonrepresentational action-perception cycles, pragmatic information, felt sense, and making sense as a sense modality, as these are explained and applied by Atmanspacher and Rickles (2022, pp. 21–37).

[3] For a detailed historical and clinical discussion of Jung's concept of the psychoid, see Addison (2019).

[4] For rich, critical discussions of archetypes, with up-to-date references, see Roesler (2022a, 2022b).

[5] The approach of Atmanspacher and Rickles (2022) similarly shows that the most basic linguistic meaning, "reference," has its source in the deeper mode of meaning expressed by the concept of "sense" (pp. 24, 36). In relation to the Pauli–Jung conjecture, Atmanspacher and Rickles see archetypes as such as constituting, and archetypal symbols as referring to, the deep structure of meaning as sense (p. 74).

[6] For fuller discussion of synchronicity and relevant references, see especially Main (2004, 2007a, 2018) as well as Chapter 2 of the present work.

[7] The possibility of noncausal explanation has been explored recently in the fields of science, mathematics, and philosophy (see Lange, 2017; Reutlinger & Saatsi, 2018).

[8] For examples of material circumstances seeming to be organized in ways that express spiritual meaning, see Main (2007a, pp. 63–140).

[9] The possibility of a form of physics incorporating the idea of the psychoid archetype (or an equivalent idea) has been demonstrated in detail by Atmanspacher and Rickles (2022) in their discussion of the variants of dual-aspect monism found in the work of Pauli and Jung, Arthur Eddington and John Wheeler, and David Bohm and Basil Hiley.

[10] A similar proposal is at the heart of Harald Walach's report for The Galileo Commission, *Beyond a Materialist Worldview: Towards an Expanded Science* (2019).

[11] This balance is theoretically implied by Jung's concept of individuation but, as Mark Saban (2019) elaborates, has not always been realized in practice, either by Jung himself or by others working within Jung's framework.

4

Metaphysics

In the previous two chapters, we looked at how Jung's psychology challenges two major presuppositions of the disenchanted worldview, namely, that there is no genuine mystery and that there is no inherent meaning. In the present chapter, we turn to the further presupposition of disenchantment that, as Egil Asprem (2014) puts it, "metaphysics is impossible" (p. 36) or, as Jason Josephson–Storm (2017) spells out, "the world is and does not represent [something else in a higher order of reality]," for "there are no truly extramundane objects or people" (p. 286). This "metaphysical scepticism," as Asprem calls it (2014, p. 36), clearly stands with the "epistemological optimism" (p. 36) of believing that all worthwhile knowledge is obtainable by empiricism and reason. It also underpins the "axiological scepticism" (p. 36) of believing that values cannot be derived from facts and hence that "science can tell us nothing about meaning" (p. 36), for one of the principal grounds for asserting that there are objective values and meanings is the historically widespread viewpoint (Seachris, 2013, p. 11) that such values and meanings are underpinned by, or even themselves are, "extramundane objects."

In philosophical literature, the term "metaphysical" is sometimes used to refer to a postulated realm of reality that transcends the empirical world (Trumble & Stevenson, 2002, p. 1759). It is primarily in this sense that the disenchanted worldview is, according to Asprem, skeptical of metaphysics. Other times, however, "metaphysical" is used to refer to attempts to provide accounts of the ultimate nature of reality, in other words, to the branch of philosophy that deals with first principles (p. 1759). Exponents of the disenchanted worldview often tend to be skeptical of being "metaphysical" in this sense too, and indeed it is not unusual, including in Jung's work, for the two senses to be conflated. Nevertheless, there is a difference between them, for in this second sense, the disenchanted view—the affirmation that the ultimate nature of reality is such that "there are no truly extramundane objects or people"—is itself clearly a metaphysical view, even though it is precisely denying the validity of metaphysical claims in the earlier sense. There will be times in the present chapter when it may be helpful to keep this distinction in mind.

Several thinkers challenging disenchantment have recognized the need to do so at a fundamental level by reexamining metaphysical assumptions (in the second sense). Morris Berman (1981), for example, attempts to replace what he calls the "modern paradigm" or "Cartesian paradigm" (p. 24), which asserts a fundamental ontological difference between mental and physical substance (*res cogitans* and *res extensa*) and has been dominant since the Scientific Revolution, with a more holistic and participative worldview (p. 23). Richard Tarnas (2006) similarly advocates for a more participatory worldview but with a focus on cosmology. Charles Taylor (2007) invokes the phenomenological thought of Martin Heidegger (1889–1976) and Maurice Merleau-Ponty (1908–61) to challenge the set of priority relations—the self as prior to external reality and the minds of others, facts as prior to values, and the natural as prior to the transcendent—that he considers naturalize and sustain the disenchanted or immanent worldview (p. 558). And Edward Kelly and colleagues (2015), using an approach similar to the one I shall apply to Jung's work, have identified a range of traditional and modern, Eastern and Western metaphysical frameworks that present radical alternatives to the materialism or physicalism commonly associated with disenchantment.

In what follows, I shall argue that Jung's thought is no less challenging of metaphysical skepticism than it is of epistemological optimism and axiological skepticism. However, since Jung often presents himself as a metaphysical skeptic, we shall first need to consider Jung's engagements with philosophy and especially with metaphysics.

JUNG AND METAPHYSICS

Jung was not a philosopher. He had read certain philosophers, such as Immanuel Kant (1724–1804), Arthur Schopenhauer (1788–1860), and Friedrich Nietzsche (1844–1900), deeply and had wide-ranging knowledge of ancient Greek, medieval, and modern European philosophy, including many noncanonical (heterodox) thinkers and traditions (see, e.g., Jung, 1921/1971a; Shamdasani, 2003, pp. 197–202). He also became familiar with some of the central tenets of Indian, Chinese, and other Eastern philosophical traditions (see, e.g., Jung, 1958/1969c; Coward, 1985, 1996; Clarke, 1994). Drawing on these and other thinkers, he concerned himself with many of the traditional problems of philosophy, such as the ultimate nature of reality, the conditions and scope of knowledge, and the question of how best to live (see, e.g., Nagy, 1991; Mills, 2019; Colacicchi, 2021). But his references to these ontological, epistemological, and ethical issues were generally subordinated to his primary aim of developing viable psychotherapeutic theory and practice. For this purpose, philosophy provided context, conceptual support, and sometimes ideas or worldviews that in specific cases were deemed to be therapeutically valuable. But philosophy was not pursued for its own sake or with the rigor one would expect from a professional philosopher. Jung stressed the close connections between philosophy and psychology, which are, he wrote, "linked by indissoluble bonds," such that "[n]either discipline can do without the other, and the one invariably furnishes the unspoken—and generally unconscious—assumptions of the other" (1931/1969b, para. 659). However, he ultimately gave precedence to his own professional field: "I always think of psychology as encompassing the whole of the psyche," he remarked, "and that includes philosophy and theology" (1916/1948/1969e, para. 525).

Relying on his understanding of Kant's critical philosophy, Jung held that metaphysical statements—by which he meant statements about realities that transcend consciousness (1949/1977c, para. 1229)—were not possible either to prove or to disprove philosophically (1955–1956/1970a, para. 667) and hence did not provide a sound basis for knowledge. Worse, the disconnection of metaphysical ideas from experience could make them not only useless but "actual impediments on the road to wider development"; for they end up as "projected contents" that are obstinately clung to despite being "ineffective, incomprehensible, and lifeless," "sterile ideas" that have lost their "true and original meaning" and relation to "living, universal psychic processes" (1951/1968b, para. 65).

For Jung metaphysical ideas were not necessarily valueless. Indeed, he affirmed that when they still retained their "root connection with natural experience" (para. 65), they could be "of the utmost importance for the well-being of the human psyche" (1945/1948/1969f, para. 568). But for this value to be realized, metaphysical assertions needed to be understood in the first instance as "statements of the psyche" and therefore as "psychological" (1935/1953/1969j, para. 835). Jung's approach to metaphysics, therefore, was to "bring everything that purports to be metaphysical into the daylight of psychological understanding"; or, put more vividly, to "strip things of their metaphysical wrappings in order to make them objects of psychology" (1929/1968d, para. 73).

Treated as psychology, metaphysical statements become experienceable, factual (1955–1956/1970a, para. 558), readable (as archetypal images) (1949/1977c, para. 1229), and hence intellectually and practically valuable (1929/1968d, para. 74). Understood psychologically, claimed Jung, metaphysics can even be a sort of "physics or physiology of the archetypes," whose "dogmas formulate the insights that have been gained into the nature of these dominants—the unconscious leitmotifs that characterize the psychic happenings of a given epoch" (1949/1977c, para. 1229).

Nor did Jung deny that metaphysical realities, that is, realities transcending consciousness, might exist and be able to impinge on human experience. He claimed to rely, in his own therapeutic work, "on the continuous influx of the numina from the unconscious and from whatever lies behind it" (1956–1957/1977h, para. 1591). Commentators who ascribed to him "an 'agnostic renunciation of all metaphysics'" were mistaken: "I merely hold that metaphysics cannot be an object of science," he responded, "which does not mean that numinous experiences do not happen frequently, particularly in the course of an analysis or in the life of a truly religious individual" (para. 1591). Indeed, Jung believed that, if there were something "ineffably metaphysical" behind metaphysical statements, his procedure of converting those metaphysical statements into psychological ones would give the metaphysical reality "the best opportunity of showing itself" (1929/1968d, para. 73). He allowed, for example, that such disclosure could take place through "the coincidence of idea and reality in the form of a special psychic state, a state of grace" (1951/1968b, para. 65). It is notable that this access to metaphysical reality that Jung deemed possible was achievable through experience and psychic states—or, at any rate, through psychophysical or synchronistic states—not through exclusively philosophical reasoning.

In sum, Jung does not deny the possible existence of a metaphysical reality, but he is wary of any claims made about such a reality that are not based on experiences amenable to psychological investigation. In fact, claims not based on experience would still be treated psychologically by Jung; they would likely be seen as symptomatic of psychic dissociation and hence as pathological. Here his prioritizing of psychology over philosophy is blatant. Metaphysics that is not treated psychologically is for Jung, we may extrapolate, at best naïve and at worst profoundly dangerous, as it can be used ideologically to provide an absolute, inscrutable warrant for any kind of personal or political action.

Abduction

The principal danger of metaphysics for Jung was thus its propensity to make claims that were not constrained by empirical reality. But there are other ways of establishing a relationship between metaphysical claims and empirical reality than Jung's proposed one of converting metaphysics into psychology. One is the process that Charles Sanders Peirce (1839-1914) called "abduction."

For Peirce, abduction was a process of inference that was neither deductive nor inductive. Whereas deduction works out the logically necessary implications of a statement and induction works out the empirically probable implications of a statement based on previous experience, abduction conjectures the most promising explanation for a statement based on what would need to be the case for that statement to be true or "a matter of course" (Peirce, 1935, p. 189). Peirce therefore described abduction as "the process of forming explanatory hypotheses," and he considered that it was "the only logical operation that introduces any new idea" (p. 172). As such, abduction for Peirce would be part of what is now often called the "context of discovery" of theories rather than part of their "context of justification" (Douven, 2011/2021, supplement on "Peirce on Abduction").

Peirce may overstate his case in the sense that the conjectured explanatory hypothesis may already exist (hence not be an entirely "new idea") before it is invoked to account for the present statement. It is also worth noting that Peirce's use of "abduction" differs from the use of the term by most contemporary philosophers for whom the process of abduction (often referred to as "inference to the best explanation") is primarily concerned with assessing the adequacy of competing theories (not with the generation of new theories) and hence is more plausibly considered part of the "context of justification" (Douven, 2011/2021, supplement on "Peirce on

Abduction"). For present purposes, however, what is important is that the concept of abduction provides an account of how there can be a relationship between an empirical state of affairs and a theory that is conjectured to account for that state of affairs, where the theory may be both metaphysical, in the sense that it includes claims that cannot themselves be empirically tested, and yet empirically constrained, in the sense that the empirical state of affairs needs to be satisfactorily explained by the theory, making the theory at least a plausible candidate for further consideration.[1]

In this chapter, I propose a metaphysical framework for understanding Jung's thought that stems from such a process of abduction. The proposal is a conjecture that appears to make particularly good sense of a wide range of problematic aspects of Jung's thought, especially those bound up in his engagement with the condition of disenchantment. To appreciate the value of this metaphysical framework, we need to view it in relation to the principal alternative framework against which it can be defined.

THE THEISTIC ROOTS OF DISENCHANTMENT

Though apparently a modern and antireligious phenomenon, disenchantment is, Weber argued, the outcome of a "great historical process in the development of religions, the elimination of magic from the world [*Entzauberung der Welt*[2]]" (1904–1905/2001, pp. 61, 178; cf. 1919/1948d, p. 138). Beginning with the Hebrew prophets and furthered by "Hellenistic scientific thought," this historical process reached its "logical conclusion" in Puritanism, which was in turn, in Weber's analysis, one of the main factors contributing to the rise of capitalism and the modern rationalization and bureaucratization of society (1904–1905/2001, p. 61; 1915/1948c, p. 350).

In relation to the role of the Hebrew prophets, Weber wrote: "The peculiar position of the old Hebrew ethic, as compared with the closely related ethics of Egypt and Babylon, and its development after the time of the prophets, rested ... entirely on this fundamental fact, the rejection of sacramental magic as a road to salvation" (1904–

1905/2001, p. 178n19). The contrast here between the Hebrew and Egyptian/Babylonian systems of ethics anticipates a distinction made by the Egyptologist Jan Assmann (2008) between "biblical monotheism" and "evolutionary monotheism." Evolutionary monotheism, as it developed in Egyptian religion for instance, is based on the idea of "the world as the embodiment of a soul-like god and of god as a soul animating the world" (Assmann, 2008, p. 273, cited in Asprem, 2014, p. 282). Such monotheism "evolves" from polytheism through the realization that ultimately "all gods are one"; as Asprem notes, it "continues to stress the co-dependence of god and the world" (2014, p. 282). By contrast, biblical monotheism, as it emerged in the Hebrew tradition and subsequently developed into what has been called "classical philosophical theism" (Clayton & Peacocke, 2004, pp. xviii, 73), results from the idea that God and the world are radically separate. As Assmann (2008) summarizes: "The Bible does not say 'All Gods are One' but rather that God is One and 'Thou shalt have no other gods ...' It does not establish a connection but rather draws a distinction between God and gods. Ultimately this distinction is one between God and world" (p. 74, cited in Asprem, 2014, p. 282).

The subsequent story of disenchantment or the progressive elimination of magic from the world has been elaborated from different perspectives by various scholars—for example, in relation to the history of Western philosophy (Tarnas, 1991/1996; 2006, pp. 16–36), the development of secularity (Taylor, 2007), and the historiography of Western esotericism (Hanegraaff, 2012; Asprem, 2014). In a nutshell: from the establishment of the exclusivist monotheism of the Bible, to the antipagan and antimagical polemics of both Catholicism and Protestantism, to the deism and rationalism of the Enlightenment, to the atheism and agnosticism of the 19th and 20th centuries, there has been overall an increasing separation of God from the world, an ever-purer sense of God's transcendence, to the point where God has been so far removed from the world of experience as to have become for many, as famously for Pierre-

Simon Laplace (1749–1827), an unnecessary hypothesis (Barbour, 1998, pp. 34–35).

From the perspective of this narrative, disenchantment, the relations between science and religion that disenchantment implies, and modern knowledge practices embedding the epistemological presuppositions of disenchantment, along with their perceived social, cultural, and environmental consequences, are constituted, albeit negatively, by the metaphysics of theism. Depending on how unnecessary the former "hypothesis" of God has become for a particular thinker, disenchantment tends to be associated either with an outright materialistic worldview or with a dualistic worldview in which the spiritual part of the dualism is beyond empirical reach. Both, the present argument suggests, are based on a metaphysics of theism.

However, alongside the development of disenchantment from theism and largely occluded by it, there has been an alternative tradition of thinking about relations between God and the world, an alternative metaphysics, in which divine immanence, including even the possibility of "enchanted" (magical and mystical) engagements with nature, has been more emphasized. This alternative tradition has come to be known over the past 200 years as panentheism.

PANENTHEISM

Panentheism is a particular view, or family of views, of the relationship between God (the divine) and the world (nature, the cosmos, the universe). Composed of the Greek words "*pan*" = all, "*en*" = in, and "*theos*" = God, the term "panentheism" means literally "a doctrine ["-*ism*"] that everything exists in God." The *Shorter Oxford English Dictionary* (Trumble & Stevenson, 2002, p. 2080) defines it as "the belief or doctrine that God includes and interpenetrates the universe while being more than it."

Panentheism was first used as a term by the German philosopher Karl Christian Friedrich Krause (1781–1832) in the 19th century (Göcke, 2018), shortly afterward receiving classic, though different, formulations in the thought of Friedrich Wilhelm Joseph von Schelling (1775–1854) and Georg Wilhelm Friedrich Hegel (1770–1831), partly in the context of debates about Baruch Spinoza's (1632–77) pantheism (Cooper, 2006, p. 67; Culp, 2008/2021). The American philosophers Charles Hartshorne and William Reese (1953/2000), especially the former, revived the term in the mid-20th century, drawing on the process philosophy of Alfred North Whitehead (1861–1947). Since then, the notion has quietly but steadily gained in influence to the point where, in the early decades of the 21st century, it has become the focus of considerable interest among Christian theologians (Clayton & Peacocke, 2004; Cooper, 2006; Brierley, 2008), process and pragmatist philosophers (Griffin, 2014; Shook, 2016; McGilchrist, 2021, pp. 1231–1239, 1248–1250), historians of Western esotericism (Hanegraaff, 2012, p. 371; Asprem, 2014, pp. 279–286), scholars of non-Christian religious traditions (Biernacki & Clayton, 2014), and researchers attempting to find adequate ways of theorizing the well-testified "rogue phenomena" of psi and mysticism (Kelly et al., 2015, pp. 536–543).

Even before the term existed, however, the idea to which it referred had long informed religious and philosophical thought not just in the West (Cooper, 2006) but also across the globe (Hartshorne & Reese, 1953/2000; Culp, 2008/2021; Biernacki & Clayton, 2014). Most influentially, though not exclusively, it is associated with currents stemming from Platonic, Neoplatonic, and Hermetic thought (Cooper, 2006, pp. 18–19; Magee, 2001, pp. 8–14). In theological terms, it relates to the evolutionary monotheism described by Assmann (2008), which stresses the connection and even coinherence and codependence of God and the world.

Just as with other views of the relationship between God and the world, panentheism is not a single, clearly defined position but rather a set of related positions. There are, therefore, several varieties of panentheism (see, for example, the discussions in Clayton, 2004b; Gregersen, 2004; Cooper, 2006; Brierley, 2008; and more critically in Thomas, 2008). Nevertheless, attempts have been made to arrive at a generic definition of the term (Clayton, 2004b, pp. 250–252; Brierley, 2008, pp. 636–641). Most helpfully for present purposes, Michael Brierley (2008) considers a range of characteristics and varieties and concludes that "panentheism's distinctiveness ... can be expressed in terms of three premises: first, that God is not separate from the cosmos [i.e., is immanent] ...; second, that God is affected by the cosmos [i.e., is passible] ...; and third, that God is more than the cosmos [i.e., is transcendent] ..." (2008, pp. 639–640).

In the light of Brierley's generic definition, panentheism can be concisely differentiated from other possible positions on the relationship between the divine and the world as follows. Unlike atheism and agnosticism, panentheism affirms the existence of the divine. Unlike theism and deism, panentheism considers the divine to be not separate from the world and even to be affected by the world (immanent and passible). And unlike pantheism, panentheism considers the divine to be more than the world (transcendent). Formulations of panentheism often stress its intermediary status between theism and pantheism. Asprem (2014), for example, describes panentheism as "a position that attempts to balance the transcendence of theism with the immanence of pantheism, while avoiding both the strict *separation* of god and nature characteristic of the former, and the *identification* of nature and god in the latter" (p. 281).

For the present discussion what is important to note is the difference between theism and panentheism.[3] Theism separates God and the world in a way that leads to disenchantment. Panentheism stresses the connection between God and the world in a way that, I shall argue, undoes disenchantment and its epistemological implications as articulated by Weber (1919/1948d) and clarified by Asprem (2014). It is my contention that Jungian psychology, albeit implicitly, is a particular instance of modern panentheistic thought and, viewed from this perspective, can be seen to open alternative ways of framing and addressing the problems that disenchantment entails.

JUNGIAN PSYCHOLOGY AS AN INSTANCE OF MODERN PANENTHEISTIC THOUGHT

There does not yet appear to have been a detailed consideration of Jung's psychology in relation to panentheism. A few previous commentators have mentioned in passing that Jung's psychology might be viewed as panentheistic, some seeing promise in this characterization (Griffin, 1989, pp. 56, 66, 245; Tacey, 2001, p. 186; 2013, p. 117), others seeing confusion (Dourley, 2014, pp. 21–22), and others again simply noting the possibility (Asprem, 2014, p. 284). But no detailed case has been made for this view, and there has also hitherto been no recognition of its importance for understanding not just Jung's conception of the relationship between science and religion but also the filiation and reception of his work.

In part, this neglect can be attributed to Jung's own vocal disclaimers that he was engaging in any form of metaphysics or theology, as well as to the fact that, when he did write about such topics, his primary purpose of amplifying psychological and psychotherapeutic insights led him to be eclectic and far from systematic. Nevertheless, postulating, abductively, that Jung's psychology is underpinned by an implicit metaphysics of panentheism seems warranted in view of the illumination it provides on both the wider intellectual contexts and the central concepts of his work.

Contextual Reasons for Viewing Jung as a Panentheist

A first indication that Jungian psychology merits consideration as a form of panentheistic thought can be found in the wider and longer history of panentheism. John Cooper, in his book *Panentheism: The Other God of the Philosophers—From Plato to the Present* (2006), has traced this history through Western religious and philosophical thought. Throughout his narrative, we continually encounter thinkers and currents of thought on which Jung either explicitly drew or which can be shown to have directly or indirectly influenced him. These thinkers and currents include Plato, Neoplatonism, Pseudo-Dionysius (5th to 6th century), John Scotus Eriugena (c. 800–c. 877), Meister Eckhart (c. 1260–c. 1328), Nicholas of Cusa (1401–1464), Jakob Boehme (1575–1624), Renaissance esotericism, early German romanticism, Friedrich Schleiermacher (1768–1834), Schelling, Hegel, Gustav Fechner (1801–87), William James, and Henri Bergson (1859–1941) (Cooper, 2006, p. 7; Jung, 1979).

In addition to thinkers who may have influenced Jung, Cooper discusses as panentheists other, contemporaneous thinkers to whom Jung does not refer but with whom scholars have subsequently considered it fruitful to compare him. These include, for example, Whitehead, Paul Tillich (1886–1965), Nikolai Berdyaev (1874–1948), and Pierre Teilhard de Chardin (1881–1955) (Cooper, 2006, p. 8; Griffin, 1989; Dourley, 2008; Nicolaus, 2010; Gustafson, 2015).

Although panentheism as a term emerged and has mostly been used in the context of recent Western thought, panentheistic dimensions and currents have also been identified within non-Western traditions, both ancient and living. In *Panentheism Across the World's Traditions* (2014) Loriliai Biernacki and Philip Clayton have assembled a set of essays that find panentheistic discourses not only within Christianity, Judaism, and Islam but also within Tibetan Buddhism, Jainism, Hinduism, and Confucianism. Jung's own cross-cultural sorties into non-Western traditions, including some of those discussed in Biernacki and Clayton's book, likewise focus on variants of them—for example, in Tibetan Buddhism, Zen Buddhism, Yoga, and Taoism (1958/1969c, paras. 759–907; 1929/1968d)—that have panentheistic characteristics.

Jung's panentheistic sources and affinities can be seen especially clearly in relation to his essay "Synchronicity: An Acausal Connecting Principle" (1952/1969r). In this essay, as we have seen, Jung proposed that a principle of acausal connection through meaning be introduced into philosophy of science as a complementary explanatory principle to that of causality. The main areas of inspiration and support on which Jung drew for the essay were precisely ones that have recently attracted intense interest in relation to panentheism. Specifically, Jung's essay drew on Western esoteric thought, including magic, divination/astrology, and alchemy (1952/1969r, paras. 859–860, 863–869, 924–936, 962; cf. Hanegraaff, 2012, p. 371; Asprem, 2014, pp. 279–286); on psychical research, parapsychology, and mind-matter research (1952/1969r, paras. 830–840, 846–857, 872–915, 949–954; cf. Asprem, 2014, pp. 287–412; Kelly et al., 2007, 2015, 2021); on Eastern thought (1952/1969r, paras. 863–866, 916–824; cf. Biernacki & Clayton, 2014); and implicitly on the project of improving dialogue between science and religion (Main, 2004, pp. 91-114; cf. Clayton & Peacocke, 2004; Kelly et al., 2015).

It is also notable that the three arguably most significant philosophical frameworks that have been invoked in recent years to illuminate Jung's concept of synchronicity and indeed Jung's psychological model generally—namely, emergence (Cambray, 2009), Whiteheadian process philosophy (Haule, 2011, pp. 173–178), and dual-aspect monism (Atmanspacher, 2012; Atmanspacher & Rickles, 2022)—have roots in or close association with panentheistic thought (Asprem, 2014, p. 245; Griffin, 2014; Kelly, 2015, p. 535). As Asprem (2014) remarks, Samuel Alexander (1859–1938) and Conway Lloyd Morgan (1852–1936), the originative emergentist thinkers, as well as Whitehead, the originative process thinker, "all seem to share a tendency towards panentheism, which stems from taking considerations of evolution, emergence, and organicism as the basis for metaphysical speculation" (p. 245). And Spinoza, the prototypical dual-aspect monist thinker, was also, as noted above, the source of the pantheism in differentiation from which Schelling's "true pantheism," that is, his panentheism, was later elaborated (Cooper, 2006, pp. 94–105).

Theoretical Reasons for Viewing Jung as a Panentheist

Most decisive, though, for confirming the panentheistic character of Jungian psychology is its fit with the three characteristics of Brierley's (2008) generic definition of panentheism: God's being not separate from the cosmos, God's being affected by the cosmos, and God's being more than the cosmos (pp. 639–640). This fit can be demonstrated especially from Jung's "Answer to Job" (1952/1969a), though also from other works.

To understand the intellectual moves Jung makes and the language he uses, it is important to appreciate that, despite his frequent disavowal of any metaphysical intentions, he effectively equated the unconscious with God: "Recognizing that [numinous experiences] do not spring from his conscious personality, [man] calls them mana, daimon, or God," he wrote, adding: "Science employs the term 'unconscious'" (1963/1995, p. 368; cf. p. 369). Jung elaborated this equation of psychological with (specifically Christian) theological concepts in a letter to the Reverend David Cox (25 September 1957):

> instead of using the term God you say "unconscious," instead of Christ "self," instead of incarnation "integration of the unconscious," instead of salvation or redemption "individuation," instead of crucifixion or sacrifice on the cross "realization of the four functions or of wholeness." I think it is no disadvantage to religious tradition if we can see how far it coincides with psychological experience. (Jung, 1956–1957/1977h, para. 1664)

Jung's apparent ontological ambiguity here is deliberate: If his statement seems to psychologize a religious concept (God), it equally sacralizes a psychological one (the unconscious) (cf. Hanegraaff, 1998, pp. 224–229). With this equation and ambiguity in mind, I note in the following how Jung's thought fits with each of the characteristics of generic panentheism first in terms of his psychological concepts and then in statements where he used the term "God" directly.

Immanence: God Is Not Separate from the World

First, in Jung's thought as in generic panentheism, God is not separate from the world. In terms of his psychological model, insofar as Jung treated the unconscious as a synonym of God and, by implication, consciousness as a synonym of the world, for him God was not essentially separate from the world, any more than the unconscious was essentially separate from consciousness (1947/1954/1969g, paras. 381–387). Similarly, the unknowable archetype, including the God archetype, was not essentially separate from the known archetypal images, including archetypal images of God (1952/1969a, paras. 557–558).

When Jung talked directly of God, he was explicit about God's nonseparation from the world, specifically from humanity: "It is ... psychologically quite unthinkable for God to be simply the 'wholly other,'" he wrote in *Psychology and Alchemy* with implicit reference to Rudolf Otto's (1917/1950) concept of the numinous, "for a 'wholly other' could never be one of the soul's deepest and closest intimacies—which is precisely what God is" (1944/1968c, para. 11n6). The nonseparation was expressed most vividly, though, in "Answer to Job," where Jung (1952/1969a) asserted: "It was only quite late that we realized (or rather, are beginning to realize) that God is Reality itself and therefore—last but not least—man" (para. 631).

Passibility: God is Affected by the World

Second, in Jung's thought as in generic panentheism, God is affected by the world. In terms of Jung's psychology, this too follows from his synonymizing of God and the unconscious. Such a relationship is suggested, for instance, by the fact that what the unconscious expresses in the form of dreams is conditioned to some extent by the attitude consciously taken toward prior dreams (1944/1968c, paras. 44–331). Similarly, in the process Jung termed "active imagination," consciously dialoguing with figures symbolizing aspects of the unconscious sometimes results in those figures— hence the unconscious—being affected by what the conscious mind has to say on its side of the dialogue (Jung, 2009/2012; 1916/1957/1969s, para. 167; 1947/1954/1969g, paras. 403; 1955–1956/1970a, paras. 705–706). More deeply, Jung considered that the constellation of archetypes in the unconscious could change (1958/1970b, para. 589; 1951/1968b), and he suggested that human efforts to become conscious could play a decisive role in such changes. As he stated at the end of his life, "just as the unconscious affects us, so the increase in our consciousness affects the unconscious" (1963/1995, p. 358).

Using the term "God" directly, Jung stated explicitly and repeatedly in "Answer to Job" that God could be affected by the creation: "Job," he argued, "by his insistence on bringing his case before God, even without hope of a hearing, had stood his ground and thus created the very obstacle that forced God to reveal his true nature" (1952/1969a, para. 584). Further: "Whoever knows God has an effect on Him" (para. 617), for "The encounter with the creature changes the creator" (para. 686). In *Memories, Dreams, Reflections,* Jung (1963/1995) suggested that through the development of human consciousness "the Creator may become conscious of His creation," such that the emergence of human consciousness could be considered "the second cosmogony" (p. 371). Even more clearly, in a letter (14 March 1953) to a correspondent who had written an essay about "Answer to Job," Jung (1976) asked rhetorically: "what in the world would be the motive of the Incarnation if man's state didn't affect God?" (p. 110)

Transcendence: God Is More than the World

Third, in Jung's thought as in generic panentheism, God is more than the world. In terms of Jung's psychological model, the unconscious is more than consciousness, and the archetype as such is not exhausted by any number of archetypal images (1947/1954/1969g, paras. 356–364, 397–420).

Using the term "God" directly in "Answer to Job," Jung (1952/1969a) was emphatic about this "more": "the image and the statement [i.e., the God-image and any statement about God] are psychic processes which are different from their transcendental object" (para. 538), he wrote. Later he asserted: "There is no doubt that there is something beyond these images that transcends consciousness" (para. 555). And he concluded "Answer to Job" with the observation that "even the enlightened person remains what he is, and is never more than his own limited ego before the One who dwells within him, whose form has no knowable boundaries, who encompasses him on all sides, fathomless as the abysms of the earth and vast as the sky" (para. 758).

Other Panentheistic Features of Jung's Thought

There are several other features of panentheistic thought, though not among those identified as generic by Brierley, which could provide points of comparison with Jungian psychology. For example, Jung's formulation of a distinction between the archetype as such and the archetypal image, as well as his notion of the archetype as having both a spiritual and an instinctual pole (1947/1954/1969g, paras. 397–420), could be compared with the dipolarity of process panentheism, which presents God as having both a primordial (eternal, unchanging) and a consequent (temporal, evolving) nature (Hartshorne & Reese, 1953/2000, pp. 1–25). Again, Jung's reflections on the transformation of the God-image (1951/1968b; 1952/1969a) could be considered in relation to the evolutionary thinking that entered modern conceptions of panentheism with Schelling and Hegel (Murphy, 2014). And the way in which Jung models consciousness as having emerged from and still being in some sense within the unconscious (1951/1968b, para. 57) has affinities with ways in which the "in" of panentheism—in what sense the world is *in* God—have been discussed (Clayton 2004b, pp. 252–253; Brierley, 2008, pp. 636–639).

Hartshorne and Reese (1953/2000) revived the concept of panentheism within theological discourse at almost exactly the same time as Jung published "Answer to Job" (1952/1969a) and "Synchronicity: An Acausal Connecting Principle" (1952/1969r). Whether Jung would have used or engaged with the concept within these works, had he been aware of it, is uncertain. He may still not have wanted to identify his implicit metaphysics (McGrath, 2014). He may have felt that too strong an endorsement of even a congenial theological position would compromise the careful balance he attempted to maintain between secular and religious perspectives (Main, 2013a; 2013c). Or the same reasons that caused him to pay scant attention to some of the most important thinkers within the history of panentheism—Spinoza, Schelling, and Hegel (Cambray, 2014, pp. 42–49; McGrath, 2014)—may have caused him also not to attend to panentheism itself. However, for the purposes of the present argument, the panentheistic character of Jungian psychology has been sufficiently established to warrant a consideration, next, of how such psychology, by virtue of being panentheistic, might undo—or break the spell of—disenchantment.

THE UNDOING OF DISENCHANTMENT

In Chapter 1, the narrative of disenchantment was shown to imply that the world has been stripped of genuine mystery, lacks inherent meaning, and is unrelated to any spiritual or divine reality—characteristics that Egil Asprem (2014) refers to more formally as epistemological optimism, axiological skepticism, and metaphysical skepticism (p. 36). Based on the preceding discussion, we can see that each of these characteristics is rendered untenable by features of Jungian psychology underpinned by an implicit panentheistic metaphysics.

Affirming Mystery

In general terms, panentheism undoes the epistemological optimism of disenchantment because the coinherence of the divine and the world, together with the divine's being more than the world, ensures that there will always remain aspects of the world that are not fully comprehensible to empiricism and reason. In other words, panentheism affirms mystery.

In the case of Jungian psychology, concepts such as those of an inexhaustible unconscious and ultimately unknowable archetypes that are continually operative on the world of experience ensure that, even in principle, reality is not fully knowable by empiricism and reason but remains replete with "mysterious incalculable forces." Jung sometimes signaled this irreducible mystery and incalculability by referring to the numinosity of the archetypes, highlighting their nature as "spiritual," "magical," and "anything but unambiguous," as well as their association with "synchronistic or parapsychic effects" (1947/1954/1969g, para. 405 and note 118). But he also expressed the idea more plainly and directly. As he wrote at the end of his life: "A man ... must sense that he lives in a world which in some respects is mysterious; that things happen and can be experienced which remain inexplicable; that not everything which happens can be anticipated. The unexpected and the incredible belong to this world. Only then is life whole. For me the world has from the beginning been infinite and ungraspable" (1963/1995, p. 390).

Affirming Inherent Meaning

In general terms, panentheism undoes axiological skepticism because part of what can be known through the empirically given (as a result of the coinherence of the divine and the world) are the values and meanings underpinned by divine immanence. In other words, panentheism affirms inherent meaning.

In the case of Jungian psychology, facts and values, far from being irreconcilably separate, are both integral to the kind of "whole judgment" that Jung's psychological model fosters (1952/1969r, para. 961; cf. 1921/1971a, para. 85; 1944/1968c, para. 20). This was prefigured in Jung's thinking about typology and became pivotal in his concept of synchronicity.

Part of Jung's typological model is its recognition of four basic functions of consciousness, which can be variously pronounced in different individuals or in the same individual at different times. Briefly, sensation perceives that a thing exists, thinking judges what it is, intuition perceives what its possibilities are, and feeling judges its value (1923/1971c, para. 900). "For complete orientation," Jung stated, conceding that this would be an ideal case, "all four functions should contribute equally" (para. 900). A whole judgment of a thing or situation thus involves not just thinking and sensation, which establish the thing or situation as a fact, but also feeling and intuition, which assess its value and wider meaning.

That these facts, values, and meanings were for Jung not just subjective constructions became clearer when he formulated his concept of synchronicity, as we saw in Chapter 3. According to synchronicity, physical events and psychic events can be connected acausally through archetypally based patterns of meaning that they jointly express (Jung, 1952/1969r). For Jung psychic properties of meaning and value can thus be as inherent in a thing or situation as the physical properties that establish it as an empirical fact. Facts and values here are complementary, ultimately inseparable aspects of the same unitary reality (see Atmanspacher & Rickles, 2022).

Affirming Spiritual and Divine Reality

If Jung was not in the end constrained by the axiological skepticism of the disenchanted perspective, neither was he constrained by its metaphysical skepticism. In general terms, panentheism undoes the metaphysical skepticism of disenchantment because the coinherence of the divine and the world allows for the possibility of knowing the divine through the empirically given—albeit not exhaustively, because of the divine's also being more than the world. In other words, panentheism affirms spiritual and divine reality.

In the case of Jungian psychology, it might seem at first that Jung shared the attitude of metaphysical skepticism. His writings, after all, are peppered with disclaimers that he was not doing metaphysics and was not a philosopher or a theologian; he was, he asserted, a scientist, an empiricist, a phenomenologist (1938/1940/1969n, para. 2; 1939/1954/1969k, paras. 759–760; 1976, p. 249). However, these disclaimers need to be seen in context. Jung was working at a time when psychology was still trying to differentiate itself from philosophy and theology, the traditional disciplines for discussing the mind and soul (Shamdasani, 2003, p. 4). Also, as we saw at the beginning of this chapter, Jung seems to have held an unnecessarily cynical view of metaphysics—if not translated into psychology—as being just baseless speculation, whereas it can, as Peirce, for example, had argued, more fruitfully be viewed in terms of abduction, that is, as a form of reasoning that infers (or intuits) on the basis of observation of phenomena the best explanation for those phenomena (Crabtree, 2015, pp. 424–447; Segal, 2014, pp. 95–96; see also McGrath, 2014).

In practice and despite his disclaimers, Jung did not treat metaphysics as impossible (Chapman, 1988; Main, 2013c; McGrath, 2014), and he found several ways by which his science could indeed "know things beyond the empirically given" (Asprem, 2014, p. 36). For one, as we saw in Chapter 2, he did not disregard phenomena whose nature and behavior were not easily reducible to established categories of empirical knowledge—phenomena variously designated as "paranormal," "anomalous," "psi," or, reflecting their growing recognition, simply "exceptional experiences" (Fach et al., 2013).[4] He allowed that such anomalousness—particularly where it seemed to involve transcendence of time, space, and causality—could be indicative of a transcendent aspect of reality (1952/1969r, paras. 912, 931, 948; 1963/1995, pp. 335–342). Throughout his life, Jung remained, as we have seen, uncommonly open to extraordinary and mystical experiences (Main, 1997; 2012; 2021).

Again, even where there was no such radical anomalousness, Jung was willing to allow that the transcendent could be known hermeneutically through its expression in the immanent. This was implicit in his understanding of the symbol as an expression of something partly known or conscious (immanent) and partly unknown or unconscious (transcendent) (1921/1971a, paras. 814–829), and of the archetypal image as a phenomenal (immanent) expression of the unknowable (transcendent) archetype as such (1947/1954/1969g, paras. 417–420).[5] But it was most clearly expressed in some of his statements about myth. Myth, for Jung, was the culturally elaborated expression of the collective unconscious and its archetypes (Segal, 1998, pp. 40–41). Through the images and narratives of myth, the unconscious could reveal archetypal truths that could not otherwise be grasped: "it is not that 'God' is a myth," wrote Jung, "but that myth is the revelation of a divine life in man. It is not we who invent myth, rather it speaks to us as a Word of God" (1963/1995, p. 373). Unlike explicit metaphysical speculation, which Jung claimed to repudiate on Kantian epistemological grounds (1976, p. 249), mythic speculation was for him empirically legitimate because it "expressed a view which springs from our psychic wholeness, from the co-operation between conscious and unconscious" (1963/1995, p. 373); not from "biased speculation" but from, as he put it, "the unfathomable law of nature herself" (1976, p. 448). In the guise of myth, he was therefore able to address numerous problems that might ordinarily be deemed metaphysical: the nature of reality (1963/1995, pp. 207–208); the origin of consciousness (pp. 284–285); the problem of evil (pp. 359–366); the meaning of life (pp. 371–372; cf. 1976, pp. 494–495); and the possibility of surviving death (1963/1995, pp. 330–358).

Jung even seemed to entertain the possibility of knowing things beyond the empirically given through a form of mystical or gnostic cognition involving participation or even unitive identification between knower and known, as we saw to some extent in Chapter 3. This is suggested by his visionary experiences following his near-fatal heart attack in 1944, as described in *Memories, Dreams, Reflections* (1963/1995, pp. 320–329; see also Main, 2021). Jung related that the various elements in these experiences—the physical environment of his hospital room, the content of his numinous visions, and his own sense of subjectivity—seemed to be "interwoven into an indescribable whole" that he was yet able to observe "with complete objectivity" (1963/1995, p. 327). He described the state of unity accessed through this "objective cognition" (p. 328) as a manifestation of the "*mysterium coniunctionis* [the mystery of the conjunction]," the "consummation" of which, he later wrote (seemingly with these experiences in mind), could "be expected only when the unity of spirit, soul, and body is made one with the original *unus mundus* [one world]" (1955–1956/1970a, para. 664) or, in psychological terms, when there was "a synthesis of the conscious with the unconscious" (para. 770). As we saw in Chapter 1, Jung characterized this conjunction as a form of mystical union (*unio mystica*), hinted at by Weber as a potential way out of disenchantment.

Reconciling Science and Spirituality

Finally, as an implication of the undoing of epistemological optimism and axiological and metaphysical skepticism, pa-nentheism also undoes the need, according to the disenchanted view, for intellectual sacrifice in order to possess religion. In general terms, this means, as we began to see in Chapter 3, that the empirical world of science is not in principle sealed off from the metaphysical world of religion: religious insights can have implications for science, and scientific insights for religion; and exploring such implications does not necessarily involve any diminution of intellectual integrity. Clearly, this is a situation conducive to dialogue and fuller reconciliation between science and religion.

In the case of Jungian psychology, such dialogue and reconciliation are exactly what we find. Insights that Jung obtained through visionary experiences, as related throughout his *Black Books* (2020) and *Red Book* (2009/2012), later provided concepts and frameworks for his scientific works (1963/1995, p. 225; Shamdasani, 2009/2012). For instance, he related that various fantasy figures with whom he conducted visionary dialogues brought home to him through these dialogues "the crucial insight that there are things in the psyche which I do not produce, but which produce themselves and have their own life" (1963/1995, p. 207)—an insight formalized in his concepts of the reality and autonomy of the psyche (1938/1940/1969n, paras. 16–18; 1952/1969a, para. 555). Conversely, data gathered in the course of his empirical work—such as the parallelisms between images in the dreams and fantasies of modern individuals and in the myths, religions, and literatures of cultures from widely differing times and places (1944/1968c)—led him to formulate concepts such as those of the collective unconscious, archetype as such, and individuation to which he was willing to accord religious significance (1938/1940/1969n; 1944/1968c).

As I have argued in detail elsewhere in relation to specific concepts, such as synchronicity, the overall tenor of Jung's work was toward increasing possibilities of dialogue and reconciliation between science and religion (Main, 2004, pp. 91–114). With that aim, Jung engaged in extended dialogues with both scientists, such as Pauli (Meier, 2001), and theologians, such as Victor White (1902–60) (Lammers & Cunningham, 2007) and Adolf Keller (1872–1963) (Jehle-Wildberger, 2020). As noted in Chapter 3, Jung even stated that he pressed for his scientific essay "Synchronicity: An Acausal Connecting Principle" (1952/1969r) and his religious essay "Answer to Job" (1952/1969a) to be published at the same time, recognizing the significant overlap or even complementarity between the issues with which they were dealing (Meier, 2001, p. 98).

In sum, in Jung's implicitly panentheistic view, far from it being necessary to sacrifice the intellect in order to possess religion, it would be one-sided not to attend to the domain of religion, at least as translated into psychological terms such as those of Jung's model, for one would thereby be denying an essential dimension of one's human wholeness. Conversely, it would be one-sided for those involved in religion not to attend to the domain of science.

PANENTHEISTIC VIS-À-VIS DISENCHANTED SCIENCE AND RELIGION

While the metaphysics of panentheism, because of its undoing of disenchantment, may be more conducive than the metaphysics of theism to dialogue and reconciliation between science and religion, it is important to note that panentheism achieves this greater dialogue and reconciliation largely by operating with heterodox understandings of science and religion. In relation to under-standings of religion, the heterodoxy is implied by the very exercise of shifting from a theistic to a panentheistic theological perspective. For example, the coinherence of the divine and the world in panentheistic religious orientations implies that humans, as part of the world, have the potential for "gnosis," that is, direct, experiential access to, and even realization of unity with, the divine in a way that has typically been considered heterodox if not heretical to adherents of theistic religions (Hanegraaff, 2012, pp. 372–373; 2016). In relation to understandings of science, the coinherence of the divine and the world in panentheism affirms both the reality and the empirical relevance of the divine and thereby makes untenable the physicalism that is almost ubiquitously presupposed within disenchanted science (Kelly et al., 2015).

It is no accident that the two works of Jung's in which evidence of implicitly panentheistic thinking can most readily be discerned, "Synchronicity: An Acausal Connecting Principle" and "Answer to Job," are both conspicuously heterodox in their principal fields. Jung's proposal, with his concept of synchronicity, that philosophy of science needs to be broadened to include a principle of acausal connection through meaning runs directly counter to the emphasis on causality and the avoidance of questions of meaning within modern science. His notion was not well received even by scientists and philosophers sympathetic to the study of anomalous phenomena (Beloff, 1977; Price, 1953). Similarly, the proposal in "Answer to Job" that the image of God in Christianity be revised to include factors that would bring it closer to the realm of human experience and make it more psychologically pertinent (factors variously identified as evil, the feminine, nature, or matter) alienated even theologians, such as White, who had been ready to collaborate with Jung (Lammers & Cunningham, 2007).

It seems that while the tension between science and religion can be considerably eased within a panentheistic framework, this may come at the cost of introducing an alternative tension: between panentheistically informed science and religion, on the one hand, and mainstream forms of science and religion informed by the perspective of disenchantment, on the other. This is not to say that attempts to promote dialogue between science and religion based on panentheistic metaphysics necessarily always involve models of science and religion that are as radically innovative as Jung's. As Kelly notes, most of the contributors to Philip Clayton and Arthur Peacocke's pioneering volume *In Whom We Live and Move and Have Our Being: Panentheistic Reflections on God's Presence in a Scientific World* (2004) explore possibilities for dialogue between "antecedently held theological views" and "conventional physicalist science, or something very close to it" (2015, p. 532). However, as Kelly has argued based on his own and his colleagues' research (Kelly et al., 2015), fuller reconciliation between science and religion might be achieved if one were to adopt "an expanded vision of science itself" together with "a full-fledged evolutionary panentheism" (Kelly, 2015, p. 532).

CONCLUSION

As noted at the beginning of this chapter, Jung, though widely read in philosophy, was not a philosopher, and any reader looking for a clear and consistent philosophical position in his work is likely to be disappointed. To take the example of the mind-body problem, Jung's published statements have been invoked to support seeing his viewpoint variously as that of idealism (Nagy, 1991; Kastrup, 2021), emergence (Hogenson, 2005; Cambray, 2009), process panpsychism (Haule, 2011), and dual-aspect monism (Atmanspacher, 2012; Atmanspacher & Rickles, 2022). Despite this diversity, however, all these framings of Jung's thought do have two important things in common: They all challenge the materialism or physicalism associated with disenchantment, and they are all in principle compatible with an overarching metaphysics of panentheism (Kelly, 2015, pp. 530–543).

Jung's lack of clarity about his philosophical position can be explained in terms of his primary orientation as a psychotherapist and his suspicion of metaphysics. As a psychotherapist, he was concerned with helping individual patients rather than with providing a consistent worldview. Being suspicious of metaphysics, he was concerned not to assert a view of reality—with all its enfolded value judgments—that was not grounded in and constrained by empirical knowledge. As we have seen, though, this fear of losing empirical grounding relates to an understanding of metaphysics that itself presupposes a certain kind of metaphysics, namely, a theistic metaphysics in which the fundamental ground or nature of reality ("God") is essentially separate from the empirical world. Panentheism precisely does not postulate such an essential separation between the ground of reality and our empirical experience of it but affirms their nonseparation and mutual transformation. The abductively conjectured metaphysics of panentheism allows for the possibility of interaction between the immanent and the transcendent, the world and its ground, and is thus not so vulnerable to Jung's objections to metaphysics. Rather, it cogently underpins a view of the world that, as Jung affirms, is genuinely mysterious, inherently meaningful, and related to spiritual and divine reality, and in which science and religion prove to be compatible.

Of course, as noted earlier, panentheism has many varieties, and it interfaces in complex and ambivalent ways with both theism and pantheism. Not all these ways are likely to fit smoothly with Jung's thought. Nevertheless, as a kind of metaphysics, panentheism has much to recommend it as a framework in which to think further about Jung's engagement with disenchantment. Since a position not implicitly underpinned by some metaphysics or other, that is, by fundamental assumptions about the nature of reality, does not appear to be possible (Walach, 2019), it is as well to make explicit and explore those metaphysical assumptions that make best sense of the widest range of data—for Jung, including the data of anomalous phenomena—and that provide support for the intuitively most satisfying ethical consequences, including the assumption that our world and our lives in the world not just are constructed as meaningful but inherently are meaningful.

ENDNOTES

1 The process of abduction played an important role in Kelly and colleagues' (2015) search for theoretical frameworks, ancient or modern, Western or Eastern, that could account adequately for their previously assembled body of "rogue" data, that is, data not readily explicable within the dominant physicalist framework of modern science and scholarship (p. 538).

2 This is the same phrase that is usually translated as "the disenchantment of the world."

3 For similarities and differences between panentheism and pantheism, see Buckareff & Nagasawa (2016) and Gilead (2021).

4 Of course, Jung considered all the phenomena he discussed, including paranormal and mystical phenomena, to be "empirical," since they were experienced and reported. His was, in the apt phrase of Edward Kelly, a "synoptic empiricism" (2015, p. 535).

5 In an open letter responding to what he saw as a mischaracterization of his work by Martin Buber (1878–1965), Jung referred to the archetypes as "immanent-transcendent" (1952/1977o, para. 1505).

Biographical note

Roderick Main, PhD, works at the University of Essex, UK, where he is a professor in the Department of Psychosocial and Psychoanalytic Studies and Director of the Centre for Myth Studies. His previous books include *The Rupture of Time: Synchronicity and Jung's Critique of Modern Western Culture* and *Revelations of Chance: Synchronicity as Spiritual Experience.*

References

Addison, A. (2019). *Jung's Psychoid Concept Contextualised*. London and New York: Routledge.

Asprem, E. (2014). *The Problem of Disenchantment: Scientific Naturalism and Esoteric Discourse 1900–1939*. Brill: Leiden, Netherlands.

Assmann, J. (2008). *Of God and Gods: Egypt, Israel, and the Rise of Monotheism*. Madison, WI: University of Wisconsin Press.

Atmanspacher, H. (2012). Dual-aspect monism à la Pauli and Jung. *Journal of Consciousness Studies, 19*, 96–120.

_____. (2021). The status of exceptional experiences in the Pauli-Jung conjecture. In R. Main, C. McMillan, & D. Henderson (Eds.), *Jung, Deleuze, and the Problematic Whole* (pp. 142–166). London: Routledge.

Atmanspacher, H., & Fach, W. (2013). A structural-phenomenological typology of mind-matter correlations. *Journal of Analytical Psychology 58*, 219–244.

Atmanspacher, H., & Rickles, D. (2022). *Dual-Aspect Monism and the Deep Structure of Meaning*. New York and London: Routledge.

Aziz, R. (1990). *C. G. Jung's Psychology of Religion and Synchronicity*. Albany, NY: State University of New York Press.

Barbour, I. (1998). *Religion and Science: Historical and Contemporary Issues*. New York: SCM Press.

Baumeister, R. (1991). *Meanings of Life*. New York: Guilford.

Beloff, J. (1977). Psi phenomena: Causal versus acausal interpretation. *Journal of the Society for Psychical Research, 49*, 573–582.

Bennett, J. (2001). *The Enchantment of Modern Life: Attachments, Crossings, and Ethics*. Princeton, NJ: Princeton University Press.

Berman, M. (1981). *The Reenchantment of the World*. Ithaca, NY: Cornell University Press.

Biernacki, L., & Clayton, P. (Eds.). (2014). *Panentheism Across the World's Traditions*. New York: Oxford University Press.

Bilgrami, A. (2010). What is enchantment? In M. Warner, J. VanAntwerpen, & C. Calhoun (Eds.), *Varieties of Secularism in a Secular Age* (pp. 145–165). Cambridge, MA: Harvard University Press.

Bishop, P. (2012). Disenchantment in education, or: "Whither art thou gone, fair world?"—Has the magic gone from the ivory tower? *International Journal of Jungian Studies*, 4, 55–69.

Blumenberg, H. (1983). *The Legitimacy of the Modern Age*. Cambridge, MA: MIT Press.

Bolen, J. S. (1979). *The Tao of Psychology: Synchronicity and the Self*. New York: Harper & Row.

Brierley, M. (2008). The potential of panentheism for dialogue between science and religion. In P. Clayton & Z. Simpson (Eds.), *The Oxford Handbook of Religion and Science* (pp. 635–651). Oxford, UK: Oxford University Press.

Broughton, R. (1991). *Parapsychology: The Controversial Science*. London: Rider.

Brown, R. (2020). *Groundwork for a Transpersonal Psychoanalysis: Spirituality, Relationship, and Participation*. London and New York: Routledge.

Buckareff, A., & Nagasawa, Y. (Eds.). (2016). *Alternative Concepts of God: Essays on the Metaphysics of the Divine*. Oxford, UK: Oxford University Press.

Cambray, J. (2009). *Synchronicity: Nature and Psyche in an Interconnected Universe*. College Station, TX: Texas A & M University Press.

_____. (2014). The influence of German romantic science on Jung and Pauli. In H. Atmanspacher & C. Fuchs (Eds.), *The Pauli-Jung Conjecture and Its Impact Today* (pp. 37–56). Exeter, UK: Imprint Academic.

Chapman, J. H. (1988). *Jung's Three Theories of Religious Experience*. Lewiston, NY: Edwin Mellen Press.

References

Charet, F. X. (1993). *Spiritualism and the Foundations of C. G. Jung's Psychology*. Albany, NY: State University of New York Press.

Clarke, J. J. (1994). *Jung and Eastern Thought: A Dialogue with the Orient*. London and New York: Routledge.

Clayton, P. (2004a). Panentheism in metaphysical and scientific perspective. In P. Clayton & A. Peacocke (Eds.), *In Whom We Live and Move and Have Our Being: Panentheistic Reflections on God's Presence in a Scientific World* (pp. 73–91). Grand Rapids, MI: Eerdmans.

_____. (2004b.). Panentheism today: A constructive systematic evaluation. In P. Clayton & A. Peacocke (Eds.), *In Whom We Live and Move and Have Our Being: Panentheistic Reflections on God's Presence in a Scientific World* (pp. 249–264). Grand Rapids, MI: Eerdmans.

Clayton, P., & Peacocke, A. (Eds.). (2004). *In Whom We Live and Move and Have Our Being: Panentheistic Reflections on God's Presence in a Scientific World*. Grand Rapids, MI: William B. Eerdmans.

Colacicchi, G. (2021). *Psychology as Ethics: Reading Jung with Kant, Nietzsche and Aristotle*. London and New York: Routledge.

Colman, W. (2011). Synchronicity and the meaning-making psyche. *Journal of Analytical Psychology, 56*, 471–491.

_____. (2012). Reply to Wolfgang Giegerich's "A serious misunderstanding: Synchronicity and the generation of meaning." *Journal of Analytical Psychology, 57*, 512–516.

Cooper, J. (2006). *Panentheism: The Other God of the Philosophers—From Plato to the Present*. Nottingham, UK: Apollos.

Coward. H. (1985). *Jung and Eastern Thought*. Albany, NY: State University of New York Press.

_____. (1996). Taoism and Jung: Synchronicity and the self. *Philosophy East and West 46*, 477–495.

Crabtree, A. (2015). Continuity of mind: A Peircean vision. In E. F. Kelly, A. Crabtree, & P. Marshall (Eds.), *Beyond Physicalism: Toward Reconciliation of Science and Spirituality* (pp. 423–453). Lanham, MD: Rowman & Littlefield.

Crawford, J. (2020). The trouble with re-enchantment. *Los Angeles Review of Books* (7 September 2020).

Culp, J. 2021. Panentheism. *The Stanford Encyclopedia of Philosophy* (Winter 2021 edition), edited by Edward N. Zalta. URL = https://plato.stanford.edu/archives/win2021/entries/panentheism /. (Original work published 2008)

Curry, P. (2019). *Enchantment: Wonder in Modern Life*. Edinburgh, UK: Floris Books.

Dawson, T. (2012). Enchantment, possession and the uncanny in E. T. A. Hoffmann's "The Sandman." *International Journal of Jungian Studies*, 4, 41–54.

de Moura, V. (2019). *Two Cases from Jung's Clinical Practice: The Story of Two Sisters and the Evolution of Jungian Analysis*. London and New York: Routledge.

Dourley, J. (2008). *Paul Tillich, Carl Jung and the Recovery of Religion*. Hove, UK: Routledge.

_____. (2014). *Jung and His Mystics: In the End It All Comes to Nothing*. London: Routledge.

Douven, I. (2021). Abduction. *The Stanford Encyclopedia of Philosophy* (E. Zalta, Ed.). https://plato.stanford.edu/archives/sum2021/entries/abduction/. (Original work published 2011)

Elms, A. (1994). The Auntification of C. G. Jung. Chapter in *Uncovering Lives: The Uneasy Alliance of Biography and Psychology* (pp. 51–70). Oxford: Oxford University Press.

Fach, W., Atmanspacher, H., Landolt, K., Wyss, T., & Rössler, W. (2013). A comparative study of exceptional experiences of clients seeking advice and of subjects in an ordinary population. *Frontiers in Psychology*, 4, 1–10.

Fellows, A. (2019). *Gaia, Psyche, and Deep Ecology: Navigating Climate Change*. London and New York: Routledge.

Flanagan, K. (1996). *The Enchantment of Sociology: A Study of Theology and Culture*. London: Macmillan.

Fordham, M. (1957). Reflections on the archetypes and synchronicity. Chapter in *New Developments in Analytical Psychology* (pp. 35–50). London: Routledge & Kegan Paul.

References

Franz, M.-L. von. (1978). The process of individuation. In C. G. Jung (Ed.), *Man and His Symbols* (pp. 157–254). London: Picador. (Original work published 1964)

_____. (1992). *Psyche and Matter*. Boston: Shambhala.

Gauchet, M. (1997). *The Disenchantment of the World: A Political History of Religion*. Princeton, NJ: Princeton University Press.

Giegerich, W. (2004). The end of meaning and the birth of man: An essay about the state reached in the history of consciousness and an analysis of C. G. Jung's psychology project. *Journal of Jungian Theory and Practice, 6*, 1–66.

_____. (2012a). The disenchantment complex: C. G. Jung and the modern world. *International Journal of Jungian Studies*, 4, 4–20.

_____. (2012b). A serious misunderstanding: Synchronicity and the generation of meaning. *Journal of Analytical Psychology*, 57, 500–511.

Gieser, S. (2005). *The Innermost Kernel: Depth Psychology and Quantum Physics. Wolfgang Pauli's Dialogue with C. G. Jung*. Berlin: Springer.

_____. (2019). Introduction. In C. G. Jung, *Dream Symbols of the Individuation Process* (S. Gieser, Ed.; pp. 1–61). Princeton, NJ: Princeton University Press.

Gilead, A. (2021). Why Spinoza was not a panentheist. *Philosophia, 49*, 2041–2051.

Göcke, B. (2018). *The Panentheism of Karl Christian Friedrich Krause (1781–1832): From Transcendental Philosophy to Metaphysics*. Berlin: Peter Lang.

Gregersen, N. (2004). Three varieties of panentheism. In P. Clayton & A. Peacocke (Eds.), *In Whom We Live and Move and Have Our Being: Panentheistic Reflections on God's Presence in a Scientific World* (pp. 19–35). Grand Rapids, MI: Eerdmans.

Griffin, D. (2014). *Panentheism and Scientific Naturalism: Rethinking Evil, Morality, Religious Experience, Religious Pluralism, and the Academic Study of Religion*. Claremont, CA: Process Century.

_____. (1988). *The Reenchantment of Science: Postmodern Proposals*. Albany, NY: State University of New York Press.

_____. (1989). *Archetypal Process: Self and Divine in Whitehead, Jung, and Hillman*. Evanston, IL: Northwestern University Press.

Gustafson, F. (Ed.). (2015). *Pierre Teilhard de Chardin and Carl Gustav Jung: Side by Side*. Cheyenne, WY: Fisher King Press.

Hanegraaff, W. (1998). *New Age Religion and Western Culture: Esotericism in the Mirror of Secular Thought*. Albany, NY: State University of New York Press.

_____. (2012). *Esotericism and the Academy: Rejected Knowledge in Western Culture*. Cambridge, UK: Cambridge University Press.

_____. (2016). Gnosis. In G. A. Magee (Ed.), *The Cambridge Handbook of Western Mysticism and Esotericism* (pp. 381–392). Cambridge: Cambridge University Press.

Harrington, A. (1996). *Reenchanted Science: Holism in German Culture from Wilhelm II to Hitler*. Princeton, NJ: Princeton University Press.

Hartshorne, C., & Reese, W. (Eds.) (2000). *Philosophers Speak of God*. New York: Humanity Books. (Original work published 1953)

Haule, J. (2011). *Jung in the 21st Century, Volume 2: Synchronicity and Science*. London: Routledge.

Heelas, P. (1996). *The New Age Movement: The Celebration of the Self and the Sacralization of Modernity*. Oxford, UK: Blackwell.

Hogenson, G. (2005). The self, the symbolic, and synchronicity: Virtual realities and the emergence of the psyche. *Journal of Analytical Psychology, 50*, 271–284.

_____. (2009). Synchronicity and moments of meeting. *Journal of Analytical Psychology, 54*, 183–197.

Homans, P. (1995) *Jung in Context: Modernity and the Making of a Psychology*. Chicago: University of Chicago Press. (Original work published 1979)

Horkheimer, M., & Adorno, T. (2002). *Dialectic of Enlightenment: Philosophical Fragments* (E. Jephcott, Trans.). Stanford, CA: Stanford University Press. (Original work published 1947)

Jaffé, A. (1970). *The Myth of Meaning in the Work of C. G. Jung*. London: Hodder & Staunton.

References

Jehle-Wildberger, M. (Ed.). (2020). *On Theology and Psychology: The Correspondence of C. G. Jung and Adolf Keller*. Princeton, NJ: Princeton University Press.

Josephson-Storm, J. (2017). *The Myth of Disenchantment: Magic, Modernity, and the Birth of the Human Sciences*. Chicago: Chicago University Press.

Jung, C. G. (1957). On the psychology and pathology of so-called occult phenomena. In H. Read et al. (Eds.), *The Collected Works of C. G. Jung: Vol. 1. Psychiatric Studies* (pp. 3–88). London: Routledge & Kegan Paul. (Original work published 1902)

_____. (1961). *The Collected Works of C. G. Jung: Vol. 4: Freud and Psychoanalysis* (H. Read et al., Eds.). London: Routledge & Kegan Paul.

_____. (1966a). On the psychology of the unconscious. In H. Read et al. (Eds.), *The Collected Works of C. G. Jung: Vol. 7. Two Essays on Analytical Psychology* (2nd ed., pp. 1–119). London: Routledge. (Original work published 1917, revised 1926 and 1943)

_____. (1966b). The psychology of the transference. In H. Read et al. (Eds.), *The Collected Works of C. G. Jung: Vol. 16. The Practice of Psychotherapy* (2nd ed., pp. 163–323). London: Routledge & Kegan Paul. (Original work published 1946)

_____. (1966c). Psychotherapy today. In H. Read et al. (Eds.), *The Collected Works of C. G. Jung: Vol. 16. The Practice of Psychotherapy* (2nd ed., pp. 94–110). London: Routledge & Kegan Paul. (Original work published 1945)

_____. (1966d). The relations between the ego and the unconscious. In H. Read et al. (Eds.), *The Collected Works of C. G. Jung: Vol. 7. Two Essays on Analytical Psychology* (2nd ed., pp. 121–241). London: Routledge. (Original work published 1928)

_____. (1966e). The structure of the unconscious. In H. Read et al. (Eds.), *The Collected Works of C. G. Jung: Vol. 7. Two Essays on Analytical Psychology* (2nd ed., pp. 269–304). London: Routledge. (Original work published 1916)

_____. (1967). *The Collected Works of C. G. Jung: Vol. 5. Symbols of Transformation* (H. Read et al., Eds.). London: Routledge & Kegan Paul. (Original work published 1911–1912, revised 1952)

_____. (1968a). Archetypes of the collective unconscious. In H. Read et al. (Eds.), *The Collected Works of C. G. Jung: Vol. 9, Pt. 1. The Archetypes and the Collective Unconscious* (2nd ed., pp. 3–41). London: Routledge & Kegan Paul. (Original work published 1934, revised 1954)

_____. (1968b). *The Collected Works of C. G. Jung: Vol. 9, Pt. 2. Aion: Researches into the Phenomenology of the Self* (2nd ed.). London: Routledge & Kegan Paul. (Original work published 1951)

_____. (1968c). *The Collected Works of C. G. Jung: Vol. 12. Psychology and Alchemy* (2nd ed.). London: Routledge & Kegan Paul. (Original work published 1944)

_____. (1968d). Commentary on "The Secret of the Golden Flower." In H. Read et al. (Eds.), *The Collected Works of C. G. Jung: Vol. 13. Alchemical Studies* (pp. 1–56). London: Routledge & Kegan Paul. (Original work published 1929)

_____. (1968e). Concerning mandala symbolism. In H. Read et al. (Eds.), *The Collected Works of C. G. Jung: Vol. 9, Pt. 1. The Archetypes and the Collective Unconscious* (2nd ed., pp. 355–384). London: Routledge & Kegan Paul. (Original work published 1950)

_____. (1968f). Conscious, unconscious, and individuation. In H. Read et al. (Eds.), *The Collected Works of C. G. Jung: Vol. 9, Pt. 1. The Archetypes and the Collective Unconscious* (2nd ed., pp. 275–289). London: Routledge & Kegan Paul. (Original work published 1939)

_____. (1968g). The psychological aspects of the Kore. In H. Read et al. (Eds.), *The Collected Works of C. G. Jung: Vol. 9, Pt. 1. The Archetypes and the Collective Unconscious* (2nd ed., pp. 182–203). London: Routledge & Kegan Paul. (Original work published 1941)

_____. (1968h). The psychology of the child archetype. In H. Read et al. (Eds.), *The Collected Works of C. G. Jung: Vol. 9, Pt. 1. The Archetypes and the Collective Unconscious* (2nd ed., pp. 151–181). London: Routledge & Kegan Paul. (Original work published 1940)

_____. (1968i). A study in the process of individuation. In H. Read et al. (Eds.), *The Collected Works of C. G. Jung: Vol. 9, Pt. 1. The Archetypes and the Collective Unconscious* (2nd ed., pp. 290–354). London: Routledge & Kegan Paul. (Original work published 1934, revised 1950)

_____. (1968j). The visions of Zosimos. In H. Read et al. (Eds.), *The Collected Works of C. G. Jung: Vol. 13. Alchemical Studies* (pp. 57–108). London: Routledge & Kegan Paul. (Original work published 1938, revised 1954)

_____. (1969a). Answer to Job. In H. Read et al. (Eds.), *The Collected Works of C. G. Jung: Vol. 11. Psychology and Religion: West and East* (2nd ed., pp. 355–470). London: Routledge & Kegan Paul. (Original work published 1952)

_____. (1969b). Basic postulates of analytical psychology. In H. Read et al. (Eds.), *The Collected Works of C. G. Jung: Vol. 8. The Structure and Dynamics of the Psyche* (2nd ed., pp. 338–357). London: Routledge & Kegan Paul. (Original work published 1931)

_____. (1969c). *The Collected Works of C. G. Jung: Vol. 11. Psychology and Religion: West and East* (2nd ed.; H. Read et al., Eds.). London: Routledge and Kegan Paul. (Original work published 1958)

_____. (1969d). Foreword to Suzuki's *Introduction to Zen Buddhism*. In H. Read et al. (Eds.), *The Collected Works of C. G. Jung: Vol. 11. Psychology and Religion: West and East* (2nd ed., pp. 538–557). London: Routledge & Kegan Paul. (Original work published 1939)

_____. (1969e). General aspects of dream psychology. In H. Read et al. (Eds.), *The Collected Works of C. G. Jung: Vol. 8. The Structure and Dynamics of the Psyche* (2nd ed., pp. 237–279). London: Routledge & Kegan Paul. (Original work published 1916, revised 1948)

_____. (1969f). On the nature of dreams. In H. Read et al. (Eds.), *The Collected Works of C. G. Jung: Vol. 8. The Structure and Dynamics of the Psyche* (2nd ed., pp. 281–297). London: Routledge & Kegan Paul. (Original work published 1945, revised 1948)

_____. (1969g). On the nature of the psyche. In H. Read et al. (Eds.), *The Collected Works of C. G. Jung: Vol. 8. The Structure and Dynamics of* the Psyche (2nd ed., pp. 159–234). London: Routledge & Kegan Paul. (Original work published 1947, revised 1954)

_____. (1969h). On synchronicity. In H. Read et al. (Eds.), *The Collected Works of C. G. Jung: Vol. 8. The Structure and Dynamics of the Psyche* (2nd ed., pp. 520–531). London: Routledge & Kegan Paul. (Original work published 1951)

_____. (1969i). A psychological approach to the dogma of the Trinity. In H. Read et al. (Eds.), *The Collected Works of C. G. Jung: Vol. 11. Psychology and Religion: West and East* (2nd ed., pp. 107–200). London: Routledge & Kegan Paul. (Original work published 1942, revised 1948)

_____. (1969j). Psychological commentary on "The Tibetan Book of the Dead." In H. Read et al. (Eds.), *The Collected Works of C. G. Jung: Vol. 11. Psychology and Religion: West and East* (2nd ed., pp. 509–526). London: Routledge & Kegan Paul. (Original work published 1935, revised 1953)

_____. (1969k). Psychological commentary on "The Tibetan Book of the Great Liberation." In H. Read et al. (Eds.), *The Collected Works of C. G. Jung: Vol. 11. Psychology and Religion: West and East* (2nd ed., pp. 475–508). London: Routledge & Kegan Paul. (Original work written 1939, published 1954)

_____. (1969m). The psychological foundation of belief in spirits. In H. Read et al. (Eds.), *The Collected Works of C. G. Jung: Vol. 8. The Structure and Dynamics of the Psyche* (2nd ed., pp. 300–318). London: Routledge & Kegan Paul. (Original work published 1920, revised 1948)

_____. (1969n). Psychology and religion. In H. Read et al. (Eds.), *The Collected Works of C. G. Jung: Vol. 11. Psychology and Religion: West and East* (2nd ed., pp. 3–105). London: Routledge & Kegan Paul. (Original work published 1938, revised 1940)

_____. (1969o). A review of the complex theory. In H. Read et al. (Eds.), *The Collected Works of C. G. Jung: Vol. 8. The Structure and Dynamics of the Psyche* (2nd ed., pp. 92–104). London: Routledge & Kegan Paul. (Original work published 1934)

_____. (1969p). The soul and death. In H. Read et al. (Eds.), *The Collected Works of C. G. Jung: Vol. 8. The Structure and Dynamics of the Psyche* (2nd ed., pp. 404–415). London: Routledge & Kegan Paul. (Original work published 1934)

_____. (1969q). The stages of life. In H. Read et al. (Eds.), *The Collected Works of C. G. Jung: Vol. 8. The Structure and Dynamics of the Psyche* (2nd ed., pp. 387–403). London: Routledge & Kegan Paul. (Original work published 1930–1931)

_____. (1969r). Synchronicity: An acausal connecting principle. In H. Read et al. (Eds.), *The Collected Works of C. G. Jung: Vol. 8. The Structure and Dynamics of the Psyche* (2nd ed., pp. 417–519). London: Routledge & Kegan Paul. (Original work published 1952)

_____. (1969s). The transcendent function. In H. Read et al. (Eds.), *The Collected Works of C. G. Jung: Vol. 8. The Structure and Dynamics of the Psyche* (2nd ed., pp. 67–91). London: Routledge & Kegan Paul. (Original work written 1916, published 1957)

_____. (1969t). Transformation symbolism in the Mass. In H. Read et al. (Eds.), *The Collected Works of C. G. Jung: Vol. 11. Psychology and Religion: West and East* (2nd ed., pp. 201–296). London: Routledge & Kegan Paul. (Original work published 1942, revised 1954)

_____. (1970a). *The Collected Works of C. G. Jung: Vol. 14. Mysterium Coniunctionis: An Inquiry into the Separation and Synthesis of Psychic Opposites in Alchemy* (2nd ed.; H. Read et al., Eds.). London: Routledge & Kegan Paul. (Original work published 1955–1956)

_____. (1970b). Flying saucers: A modern myth of things seen in the skies. In H. Read et al. (Eds.), *The Collected Works of C. G. Jung: Vol. 10. Civilization in Transition* (2nd ed., pp. 307–433). London: Routledge & Kegan Paul. (Original work published 1958)

_____. (1970c). The meaning of psychology for modern man. In H. Read et al. (Eds.), *The Collected Works of C. G. Jung: Vol. 10. Civilization in Transition* (2nd ed., pp. 134–156). London: Routledge & Kegan Paul. (Original work published 1933, revised 1934)

_____. (1970d). The spiritual problem of modern man. In H. Read et al. (Eds.), *The Collected Works of C. G. Jung: Vol. 10. Civilization in Transition*

(2nd ed., pp. 74–94). London: Routledge & Kegan Paul. (Original work published 1928, revised 1931)

_____. (1970e). The undiscovered self (present and future). In H. Read et al. (Eds.), *The Collected Works of C. G. Jung: Vol. 10. Civilization in Transition* (2nd ed., pp. 245–305). London: Routledge & Kegan Paul. (Original work published 1957)

_____. (1971a). *The Collected Works of C. G. Jung: Vol. 6: Psychological Types* (2nd ed., H. Read et al., Eds.). London: Routledge & Kegan Paul. (Original work published 1921)

_____. (1971b). A contribution to the study of psychological types. In H. Read et al. (Eds.), *The Collected Works of C. G. Jung: Vol. 6: Psychological Types* (2nd ed., pp. 499–509). London: Routledge & Kegan Paul. (Original work published 1913)

_____. (1971c). Psychological types. In H. Read et al. (Eds.), *The Collected Works of C. G. Jung: Vol. 6: Psychological Types* (2nd ed., pp. 510–523). London: Routledge & Kegan Paul. (Original work published 1923)

_____. (1973a). *C. G. Jung Letters: Vol. 1. 1906–1950* (G. Adler, Ed.). London: Routledge.

_____. (1973b). *The Collected Works of C. G. Jung: Vol. 2: Experimental Researches* (H. Read et al., Eds.). London: Routledge & Kegan Paul.

_____. (1976). *C. G. Jung Letters: Vol. 2. 1951–1961* (G. Adler, Ed.). London: Routledge.

_____. (1977a). Adaptation, individuation, collectivity. In H. Read et al. (Eds.), *The Collected Works of C. G. Jung: Vol. 18. The Symbolic Life* (pp. 449–454). London: Routledge & Kegan Paul. (Original work written 1916)

_____. (1977b). An astrological experiment. In H. Read et al. (Eds.), *The Collected Works of C. G. Jung: Vol. 18. The Symbolic Life* (pp. 494–501). London: Routledge & Kegan Paul. (Original work published 1958)

_____. (1977c). Foreword to Harding: "Women's Mysteries." In H. Read et al. (Eds.), *The Collected Works of C. G. Jung: Vol. 18. The Symbolic Life* (pp. 518–520). London: Routledge & Kegan Paul. (Original work published 1949)

____. (1977d). Foreword to Jaffé: *Apparitions and Precognition*. In H. Read et al. (Eds.), *The Collected Works of C. G. Jung: Vol. 18. The Symbolic Life* (pp. 327–329). London: Routledge & Kegan Paul. (Original work published 1957)

____. (1977e). Foreword to Jung: *Phénomènes occultes*. In H. Read et al. (Eds.), *The Collected Works of C. G. Jung: Vol. 18. The Symbolic Life* (pp. 309–311). London: Routledge & Kegan Paul. (Original work published 1938)

____. (1977f). Foreword to Moser: "Spuk: Irrglaube oder Wahglaube?" In H. Read et al. (Eds.), *The Collected Works of C. G. Jung: Vol. 18. The Symbolic Life* (pp. 317–326). London: Routledge & Kegan Paul. (Original work published 1950)

____. (1977g). The future of parapsychology. In H. Read et al. (Eds.), *The Collected Works of C. G. Jung: Vol. 18. The Symbolic Life* (pp. 510–511). London: Routledge & Kegan Paul. (Original work published 1960)

____. (1977h). Jung and religious belief. In H. Read et al. (Eds.), *The Collected Works of C. G. Jung: Vol. 18. The Symbolic Life* (pp. 702–744). London: Routledge & Kegan Paul. (Original work published 1956–1957)

____. (1977i). Letters on synchronicity. In H. Read et al. (Eds.), *The Collected Works of C. G. Jung: Vol. 18. The Symbolic Life* (pp. 293–308). London: Routledge & Kegan Paul. (Original work published 1950–1955)

____. (1977j). Marginalia on contemporary events. In H. Read et al. (Eds.), *The Collected Works of C. G. Jung: Vol. 18. The Symbolic Life* (pp. 591–603). London: Routledge & Kegan Paul. (Original work published 1945)

____. (1977k). On flying saucers. In H. Read et al. (Eds.), *The Collected Works of C. G. Jung: Vol. 18. The Symbolic Life* (pp. 626–633). London: Routledge & Kegan Paul. (Original work published 1954)

____. (1977m). On spiritualistic phenomena. In H. Read et al. (Eds.), *The Collected Works of C. G. Jung: Vol. 18. The Symbolic Life* (pp. 293–308). London: Routledge & Kegan Paul. (Original work published 1905)

____. (1977n). Psychology and spiritualism. In H. Read et al. (Eds.), *The Collected Works of C. G. Jung: Vol. 18. The Symbolic Life* (pp. 312–316). London: Routledge & Kegan Paul. (Original work published 1948)

_____. (1977o). Religion and psychology: A reply to Martin Buber. In H. Read et al. (Eds.), *The Collected Works of C. G. Jung: Vol. 18. The Symbolic Life* (pp. 663–670). London: Routledge & Kegan Paul. (Original work published 1952)

_____. (1977p). The symbolic life. In H. Read et al. (Eds.), *The Collected Works of C. G. Jung: Vol. 18. The Symbolic Life* (pp. 265–290). London: Routledge & Kegan Paul. (Original work published 1939)

_____. (1977q). Symbols and the interpretation of dreams. In H. Read et al. (Eds.), *The Collected Works of C. G. Jung: Vol. 18. The Symbolic Life* (pp. 183–264). London: Routledge & Kegan Paul. (Original work published 1961)

_____. (1977r). The Tavistock lectures: On the theory and practice of analytical psychology. In H. Read et al. (Eds.), *The Collected Works of C. G. Jung: Vol. 18. The Symbolic Life* (pp. 626–633). London: Routledge & Kegan Paul. (Original work published 1935)

_____. (1979). *The Collected Works of C. G. Jung: Vol. 20. General Index* (B. Forryan & J. Glover, Compiled.). London: Routledge & Kegan Paul.

_____. (1983). *The Collected Works of C. G. Jung: Supplementary Vol. A: The Zofingia Lectures*. Princeton, NJ: Princeton University Press. (Original work written 1896–1899)

_____. (1990). *Analytical Psychology: Notes of the Seminar Given in 1925* (W. McGuire, Ed.). London: Routledge.

_____. (1991). *Psychology of the Unconscious: A Study of the Transformations and Symbolisms of the Libido* (B. Hinkle, Trans.). Princeton, NJ: Princeton University Press. (Original work published 1911–1912, translated 1919)

_____. (1995). *Memories, Dreams, Reflections* (A. Jaffé, Ed.). London: Fontana. (Original work published 1963)

_____. (2012). *The Red Book: Liber Novus. A Reader's Edition.* (S. Shamdasani, Ed.). New York: Norton. (Original work published 2009)

_____. (2020). *The Black Books 1913–1932: Notebooks of Transformation* (Vols. 1–7; S. Shamdasani, Ed.). New York: Norton.

_____. (Ed.). (1978). *Man and His Symbols*. London: Picador. (Original work published 1964)

Jung, C. G., & Pauli, W. (1955). *The Interpretation of Nature and the Psyche* (R. F. C. Hull & P. Silz, Trans.). London: Routledge & Kegan Paul. (Original work published 1952)

Jung, E., & von Franz, M.-L. (1980). *The Grail Legend*. Boston, MA: Sigo/ London: Coventure. (Original work published 1970)

Kastrup, B. (2021). *Decoding Jung's Metaphysics: The Archetypal Semantics of an Experiential Universe*. Alresford, UK: Iff Books.

Kelly, E. F. (2015). Toward a worldview grounded in science *and* spirituality. In Kelly et al. (Eds.), *Beyond Physicalism: Toward Reconciliation of Science and Spirituality* (pp. 493–551). Lanham, MD: Rowman & Littlefield.

Kelly, E. F., Kelly, E. W., Crabtree, A., Gould, A., Grosso, M., & Greyson, B. (2007). *Irreducible Mind: Toward a Psychology for the 21st Century*. Lanham, MD: Rowman & Littlefield.

Kelly, E. F., Crabtree, A., & Marshall, P. (Eds.). (2015). *Beyond Physicalism: Toward Reconciliation of Science and Spirituality*. Lanham, MD: Rowman & Littlefield.

Kelly, E. F., & Marshall, P. (Eds.). (2021). *Consciousness Unbound: Liberating Mind from the Tyranny of Materialism*. Lanham, MD: Rowman & Littlefield.

Kelly, S. (1993). *Individuation and the Absolute: Hegel, Jung, and the Path Toward Wholeness*. New York: Paulist Press.

Kime, P. (2019). Synchronicity and meaning. *Journal of Analytical Psychology, 64*, 780–797.

Kingsley, P. (2018). *Catafalque: Carl Jung and the End of Humanity* (Vols. 1–2). London: Catafalque Press.

Koestler, A. (1972). *The Roots of Coincidence*. London: Hutchinson.

Kripal, J. (2011). *Mutants and Mystics: Science Fiction, Superhero Comics, and the Paranormal*. Chicago: University of Chicago Press.

Kripal, J., with Jain, A. Prophet, E., & Anzali, A. (2014). *Comparing Religions*. Oxford, UK: Wiley–Blackwell.

Lammers, A., & Cunningham, A. (Eds.). (2007). *The Jung-White Letters*. Hove, UK: Routledge.

Landy, J., & Saler, M. (Eds.). (2009). *The Re-Enchantment of the World: Secular Magic in a Rational Age*. Stanford, CA: Stanford University Press.

Lange, M. (2017). *Because Without Cause: Non-Causal Explanations in Science and Mathematics*. Oxford, UK: Oxford University Press.

Liebscher, M. (Ed.). (2015). *Analytical Psychology in Exile: The Correspondence of C. G. Jung and Erich Neumann*. Princeton, NJ: Princeton University Press.

Magee, G. A. (2001). *Hegel and the Hermetic Tradition*. Ithaca, NY: Cornell University Press.

Main, R. (2004). *The Rupture of Time: Synchronicity and Jung's Critique of Modern Western Culture*. Hove, UK: Brunner-Routledge.

_____. (2007a). *Revelations of Chance: Synchronicity as Spiritual Experience*. Albany, NY: State University of New York Press.

_____. (2007b). Synchronicity and analysis: Jung and after. *European Journal of Psychotherapy and Counselling, 9*, 359-71.

_____. (2011). Synchronicity and the limits of re-enchantment. *International Journal of Jungian Studies, 3*, 144–158.

_____. (2012). Anomalous phenomena, synchronicity, and the re-sacralization of the modern world. In S. Kakar & J. Kripal (Eds.), *Seriously Strange: Thinking Anew about Psychical Experiences* (pp. 1–27, 275–283). New Delhi, India: Penguin.

_____. (2013a). In a secular age: Weber, Taylor, Jung. *Psychoanalysis, Culture & Society, 18*, 277–294.

_____. (2013b). Myth, synchronicity, and re-enchantment. In L. Burnett, S. Bahun, & R. Main (Eds.), *Myth, Literature, and the Unconscious* (pp. 129–146). London: Karnac.

_____. (2013c). Secular *and* religious: The intrinsic doubleness of analytical psychology and the hegemony of naturalism in the social sciences. *Journal of Analytical Psychology, 58*, 366–386.

_____. (2014). Synchronicity and the problem of meaning in science. In H. Atmanspacher & C. Fuchs (Eds.), *The Pauli-Jung Conjecture and Its Impact Today* (pp. 217–239). Exeter, UK: Imprint Academic.

References

____. (2015). Psychology and the occult: Dialectics of disenchantment and re-enchantment in the modern self. In C. Partridge (Ed.), *The Occult World* (pp. 732–743). London and New York: Routledge.

____. (2017). Panentheism and the undoing of disenchantment. *Zygon, 52,* 1098–1122.

____. (2019). Synchronicity and holism. *Analytical Psychology Meets Academic Research: Avignon Conference 2018, Revue de Psychologie Analytique* (Hors série), 59–74.

____. (2021a). The ethical ambivalence of holism: An exploration through the thought of Carl Jung and Gilles Deleuze. In R. Main, C. McMillan, & D. Henderson (Eds.), *Jung, Deleuze, and the Problematic Whole* (pp. 20–50). London and New York: Routledge.

____. (2021b). Mystical experience and the scope of C. G. Jung's holism. In E. F. Kelly & P. Marshall (Eds.), *Consciousness Unbound: Liberating Mind from the Tyranny of Materialism* (pp. 139–174). Lanham, MD: Rowman & Littlefield.

____. (Ed.). (1997). *Jung on Synchronicity and the Paranormal*. London: Routledge.

Main, R., McMillan, C., & Henderson, D. (Eds.). (2021). *Jung, Deleuze, and the Problematic Whole*. London: Routledge.

Mansfield, V. (1995). *Synchronicity, Science, and Soul-Making: Understanding Jungian Synchronicity through Physics, Buddhism, and Philosophy*. Chicago: Open Court.

____. (2002). *Head and Heart: A Personal Exploration of Science and the Sacred*. Wheaton, IL: Quest Books.

Mansfield, V., Rhine-Feather, S., & Hall, J. (1998). The Rhine-Jung letters: Distinguishing synchronicity from parapsychological phenomena. *Journal of Parapsychology, 62,* 3–25.

Mathers, D. (2001). *An Introduction to Meaning and Purpose in Analytical Psychology*. Hove, UK and Philadelphia, PA: Brunner-Routledge.

McGilchrist, I. (2021). *The Matter with Things: Our Brains, Our Delusions, and the Unmaking of the World* (Vols. 1–2). London: Perspectiva.

McGrath, S. (2014). The question concerning metaphysics: A Schellingian intervention in analytical psychology. *International Journal of Jungian Studies, 6*, 23–51.

McGuire, W. (Ed.). (1974). *The Freud/Jung Letters: The Correspondence between Sigmund Freud and C. G. Jung* (R. Manheim & R. F. C. Hull, Trans.). Princeton, NJ: Princeton University Press.

McGuire, W., & Hull, R. F. C. (Eds.). (1978). *C. G. Jung Speaking: Interviews and Encounters*. London: Thames & Hudson.

McMillan, C., Main, R., & Henderson, D. (Eds.). (2020). *Holism: Possibilities and Problems*. London and New York: Routledge.

Meier, C. A. (Ed.). (2001). *Atom and Archetype: The Pauli/Jung Letters 1932–1958*. London: Routledge.

Meijer, M., & De Vriese, H. (Eds.). (2021). *The Philosophy of Reenchantment*. London and New York: Routledge.

Miller, A. (2009). *Deciphering the Cosmic Number: The Strange Friendship of Wolfgang Pauli and Carl Jung*. New York: Norton.

Mills, J. (Ed.). (2019). *Jung and Philosophy*. London and New York: Routledge.

Moore, T. (1996). *The Re-Enchantment of Everyday Life*. New York: Harper-Collins.

Murphy, M. (2014). The emergence of evolutionary panentheism. In L. Biernacki & P. Clayton (Eds.), *Panentheism Across the World's Traditions* (pp. 177–199). Oxford, UK: Oxford University Press.

Nagy, M. (1991). *Philosophical Issues in the Psychology of C. G. Jung*. Albany, NY: State University of New York Press.

Neumann, E. (1954). *The Origins and History of Consciousness*. London: Routledge & Kegan Paul.

_____. (1955). *The Great Mother: Analysis of an Archetype*. London: Routledge & Kegan Paul.

Nicolaus, G. (2010). *C. G. Jung and Nikolai Berdyaev: Individuation and the Person: A Critical Comparison*. Hove, UK and New York: Routledge.

Oeri, A. (1970). Some youthful memories of C. G. Jung. *Spring: An Annual of Archetypal Psychology and Jungian Thought*, 182–189.

Otto, R. (1950). *The Idea of the Holy* (2nd ed.; J. Harvey, Trans.). Oxford, UK: Oxford University Press. (Original work published 1917)

References

Paloutzian, R., & Park, C. (2013). Recent progress and core issues in the science of the psychology of religion and spirituality. In R. Paloutzian & C. Park (Eds.), *Handbook of the Psychology of Religion and Spirituality* (2nd ed.; pp. 3–22). New York: The Guildford Press.

Partridge, C. (2004). *The Re-Enchantment of the West, Volume 1: Alternative Spiritualities, Sacralization, Popular Culture and Occulture*. Edinburgh, UK: T & T Clark.

_____. (2014). Occulture is ordinary. In E. Asprem & K. Granholm (Eds.), *Contemporary Esotericism* (pp. 113–133). London and New York: Routledge.

Pauli, W. (1955). The influence of archetypal ideas on the scientific theories of Kepler (P. Silz, Trans.). In C. G. Jung & W. Pauli, *The Interpretation of Nature and the Psyche* (pp. 147–240). New York: Pantheon. (Original work published 1952)

_____. (2002). The piano lesson: An active fantasy about the unconscious (F. W. Wiegel, H. van Erkelens, & J. van Meurs, Trans.). *Harvest: Journal for Jungian Studies*, *48*, 122–134.

Peirce, C. S. (1935). *Collected Papers of Charles Sanders Peirce, Vols. V and VI: Pragmatism and Pragmaticism and Scientific Metaphysics* (C. Hartshorne & P. Weiss, Eds.). Cambridge, MA: Harvard University Press.

Price, H. H. (1953). Review of Carl Gustav Jung and Wolfgang Pauli, *Naturerklärung und Psyche*. *Journal of the Society for Psychical Research 37*, 26–35.

Radin, D. (1997). *The Conscious Universe: The Scientific Truth of Psychic Phenomena*. New York: HarperCollins.

Radkau, J. (2009). *Max Weber: A Biography* (P. Camiller, Trans.). Cambridge, UK: Polity. (Original work published 2005)

Reutlinger, A., & Saatsi, J. (Eds.) (2018). *Explanation Beyond Causation: Philosophical Perspectives on Non-Causal Explanations*. Oxford, UK: Oxford University Press.

Roesler, C. (2022a). *C. G. Jung's Archetype Concept: Theory, Research and Applications*. London and New York: Routledge.

_____. (2022b). Development of a reconceptualization of archetype theory: Report to the IAAP. Zurich: International Association of Analytical Psychology.

Russell, B. (2013). A free man's worship. In J. Seachris (Ed.), *Exploring the Meaning of Life: An Anthology and Guide* (pp. 230–235). Oxford, UK: Wiley–Blackwell. (Original work published 1903)

Saban, M. (2012). The dis/enchantment of C. G. Jung. *International Journal of Jungian Studies, 4*, 21–33.

_____. (2019). *"Two Souls Alas": Jung's Two Personalities and the Making of Analytical Psychology*. Asheville, NC: Chiron Publications.

Samuels, A., Shorter, B., & Plaut, F. (1986). *A Critical Dictionary of Jungian Analysis*. London and New York: Routledge.

Seachris, J. (Ed.) (2013). *Exploring the Meaning of Life: An Anthology and Guide*. Oxford, UK: Wiley–Blackwell.

Seager, W. (2009). A new idea of reality: Pauli on the unity of mind and matter. In H. Atmanspacher & H. Primas (Eds.), *Recasting Reality: Wolfgang Pauli's Philosophical Ideas and Contemporary Science* (pp. 83–97). Berlin: Springer.

Segal, R. (2014). Explanation and interpretation. In R. Jones (Ed.), *Jung and the Question of Science* (pp. 82–97). London and New York: Routledge.

_____. (Ed.). (1992). *The Gnostic Jung*. Princeton, NJ: Princeton University Press.

_____. (Ed.). (1998). *Jung on Mythology*. London: Routledge.

Shamdasani, S. (1995). Memories, dreams, omissions. *Spring: Journal of Archetype and Culture, 57*, 115–137.

_____. (2003). *Jung and the Making of Modern Psychology: The Dream of a Science*. Cambridge, UK: Cambridge University Press.

_____. (2012). *Liber Novus*: The "Red Book" of C. G. Jung. In C. G. Jung, *The Red Book: Liber Novus: A Reader's Edition* (S. Shamdasani, Ed.; pp. 1–95). New York: W. W. Norton. (Original work published 2009)

_____. (2020). Toward a visionary science: Jung's notebooks of transformation. In C.G. Jung, *The Black Books 1913–1932: Notebooks of Transformation* (Vols. 1–7; S. Shamdasani, Ed.; Vol. 1, pp. 11–112). New York: Norton.

Sherry, P. (2009). Disenchantment, re-enchantment, and enchantment. *Modern Theology, 25*, 369–386.

Shook, J. (2016). Panentheism and Peirce's God: Theology guided by philosophy and cosmology. *Philosophy, Theology, and the Sciences, 3*, 8–31.

Smith, C. (1990). *Jung's Quest for Wholeness: A Religious and Historical Perspective*. Albany, NY: State University of New York Press.

Stein, M. (2006). Individuation. In R. Papadopoulos (ed.), *The Handbook of Jungian Psychology: Theory, Practice and Applications* (pp. 196–214). London and New York: Routledge.

_____. (2014). Minding the self. In *Minding the Self: Jungian Meditations on Contemporary Spirituality* (pp. 111–126). London: Routledge.

_____. (2019). Psychological individuation and spiritual enlightenment: some comparisons and points of contact. *Journal of Analytical Psychology 64*, 6–22.

Sutcliffe, S., & Gilhus, I. (2014). *New Age Spirituality: Rethinking Religion*. London: Routledge.

Tacey, D. (2001). *Jung and the New Age*. Hove, UK, and New York: Brunner-Routledge.

_____. (2013). *The Darkening Spirit: Jung, Spirituality, Religion*. London and New York: Routledge.

Tarnas, R. (1996). *The Passion of the Western Mind: Understanding the Ideas that Have Shaped Our World View*. London: Pimlico. (Original work published 1991)

_____. (2006). *Cosmos and Psyche: Intimations of a New World View*. London: Penguin.

Taylor, C. (2007). *A Secular Age*. Cambridge, MA: Harvard University Press.

Thomas, O. (2008). Problems in panentheism. In P. Clayton & Z. Simpson (Eds.), *The Oxford Handbook of Religion and Science* (pp. 652–664). Oxford: Oxford University Press.

Trumble, W., & Stevenson, A. (Eds.). (2002). *Shorter Oxford English Dictionary* (5th ed.). Oxford, UK: Oxford University Press.

Walach, H. (2019). *Beyond a Materialist Worldview: Towards an Expanded Science*. London: Scientific and Medical Network.

Weber, M. (1948a). Bureaucracy. In H. Gerth & C. Wright Mills (Eds.), *From Max Weber: Essays in Sociology* (pp. 196–244). New York: Oxford University Press. (Original work published 1922)

_____. (1948b). Politics as a vocation. In H. Gerth & C. Wright Mills (Eds.), *From Max Weber: Essays in Sociology* (pp. 78–128). New York: Oxford University Press. (Original work published 1919)

_____. (1948c). Religious rejections of the world and their directions. In H. Gerth & C. Wright Mills (Eds.), *From Max Weber: Essays in Sociology* (pp. 323–359). New York: Oxford University Press. (Original work published 1915)

_____. (1948d). Science as a vocation. In H. Gerth & C. Wright Mills (Eds.), *From Max Weber: Essays in Sociology* (pp. 129–156). New York: Oxford University Press. (Original work published 1919)

_____. (1952a). *Ancient Judaism* (H. Gerth, Trans.). Glencoe, IL: The Free Press. (Original work published 1917–1919)

_____. (1952b). *The Religion of China: Confucianism and Taoism* (H. Gerth, Trans.). Glencoe, IL: The Free Press. (Original work published 1915)

_____. (1958). *The Religion of India: The Sociology of Hinduism and Buddhism* (H. Gerth & D. Martindale, Trans.). Glencoe, IL: The Free Press. (Original work published 1916)

_____. (2001). *The Protestant Ethic and the Spirit of Capitalism*. London and New York: Routledge. (Original work published 1904–1905)

_____. (2019). *Economy and Society: A New Translation* (K. Tribe, Ed. and Trans.). Cambridge, MA: Harvard University Press. (Original work published 1922)

Whan, M. (2012). Myth, disenchantment and the loss of sacred place. *International Journal of Jungian Studies*, 4, 34–40.

Williams, M. (1963). The indivisibility of the personal and collective unconscious. *Journal of Analytical Psychology 8*, 45–50.

Yelle, R., & Trein, L. (Eds.). (2021). *Narratives of Disenchantment and Secularization: Critiquing Max Weber's Idea of Modernity*. London: Bloomsbury Academic.

Index

Index

Lévy-Bruhl, Lucien 17

magic 3, 9, 20, 25, 31, 32, 38, 107, 108, 114

mandalas 38, 60

materialism 7, 42, 102, 128

meaning 2, 4, 6, 7, 9, 11, 18, 25, 26, 33, 36–39, 42–44, 53, 58–60, 64, 65, 71–92, 94, 96, 97–99, 101, 104, 113, 119–121, 123, 126, 127

metaphysical skepticism 103, 119, 121, 122, 124

metaphysics 12, 14, 101, 103–106, 109, 112, 119, 122, 126, 127–129

modernity 5, 7, 13, 38, 42, 63, 66, 97, 70, 90

monotheism 108, 110, 113

Moore, Thomas 30

mysterium coniunctionis 16, 19, 22, 25, 31, 124

mystery 3–7, 11, 25, 29, 36–38, 41, 65, 101, 119, 120, 124

mysticism 11, 32–35, 110

myth 13, 38, 66, 68, 123

Neoplatonism 113

Nietzsche, Friedrich 103

numinosity 7, 52, 70, 79, 98, 120

Otto, Rudolf 66

panpsychism 54, 55

pantheism 110, 111, 114, 129, 130

panentheism 109–122, 126–130

parapsychology 42, 84, 114

participation 17, 20, 39, 123

Pauli, Wolfgang 7, 12, 54, 57, 58, 69, 73–75, 82, 83, 90–95, 97–99, 125

Peacocke, Arthur 108, 110, 114

Peirce, Charles Sanders 106, 122

Philemon 31, 38, 48, 56, 61, 63

philosophy 39, 55, 84, 87, 90, 91, 99, 102–105, 108, 110, 113, 114, 122, 126, 127

physics 4, 74, 82–84, 92–95, 99, 104

Plato 72, 112, 113

polytheism 2, 108

precognition 54

Protestantism 34, 108

Pseudo-Dionysius 113

psyche 12, 13, 15, 17, 20–22, 27, 39, 52, 55, 56, 64, 73, 77, 82, 85, 91–95, 104, 125

psychical research 11, 42–45, 57, 114

psychoid archetype 82, 83, 90, 92, 96, 99

psychokinesis 54, 55

psychological types 1

psychology 2, 5, 6, 7, 12–14, 16, 32, 37, 42–44, 63, 65, 68, 69, 71, 75, 78, 82, 83, 89, 90, 92–96, 101, 103–106, 111, 112, 115, 116, 118–120, 122, 125

psychosocial 16, 17, 37

rationalization 3, 8, 9, 14, 35, 41, 63, 73, 74, 107

reanimation 61, 66

rebirth 52, 80, 81, 89

Red Book 1, 5, 6, 36, 94, 125

reenchantment 10–12, 14, 16, 18–20, 22–25, 27–32, 36, 38–40, 75, 97

Reese, Wiliam 110, 118, 119

Reich, Wilhelm 12

Reichstein, Maggie 7

Rhine, Joseph Banks 42, 45, 49, 54

religion 4, 5, 7, 10, 11, 25, 26, 29, 32, 33, 35, 38, 78, 92, 93, 108, 109, 112, 114, 124–127, 129

Rickles, Dean 70, 75, 96–99, 114, 121, 128

Saban, Mark 13, 65, 99

Printed in the USA
CPSIA information can be obtained
at www.ICGtesting.com
LVHW090524240923
758931LV00002B/399